EVANGELIZING THE DEPTHS

EVANGELIZING *the* DEPTHS

A Pathway to Inner Unity

Simone Pacot

Translated from the French by
Roger W. T. Wilkinson

CASCADE *Books* · Eugene, Oregon

EVANGELIZING THE DEPTHS
A Pathway to Inner Unity

Copyright © 2018 Simone Pacot. All rights reserved. Except for brief quotations in critical publications or reviews, no part of this book may be reproduced in any manner without prior written permission from the publisher. Write: Permissions, Wipf and Stock Publishers, 199 W. 8th Ave., Suite 3, Eugene, OR 97401.

Cascade Books
An Imprint of Wipf and Stock Publishers
199 W. 8th Ave., Suite 3
Eugene, OR 97401

www.wipfandstock.com

PAPERBACK ISBN: 978-1-5326-4506-8
HARDCOVER ISBN: 978-1-5326-4507-5
EBOOK ISBN: 978-1-5326-4508-2

Cataloguing-in-Publication data:

Names: Pacot, Simone, author. | Wilkinson, Roger W. T., translator

Title: Evangelizing the depths : a pathway to inner unity / Simone Pacot ; translated by Roger W. T. Wilkinson.

Description: Eugene, OR: Cascade Books, 2018 | Includes bibliographical references.

Identifiers: ISBN 978-1-5326-4506-8 (paperback) | ISBN 978-1-5326-4507-5 (hardcover) | ISBN 978-1-5326-4508-2 (ebook)

Subjects: LCSH: Spiritual life—Christianity | Spiritual formation | Christianity—Psychology | Suffering | Healing | Bible—Devotional use | Forgiveness

Classification: BV4511 P11 2018 (print) | BV4511 (ebook)

Manufactured in the U.S.A.   SEPTEMBER 25, 2018

CONTENTS

CONTENTS

TRANSLATOR'S NOTE

It is hoped that the translation of this fine book will not impede its reading! There are a few terms in French which do not sound right when translated into their direct cognates, and in particular the translation has avoided using "human being," preferring "human person" or "people"; French is happier in the use of what is now thought of as gender exclusive language, and an effort has been made to soften this. Occasional notes are provided on nicer points of translation; these notes are alongside those of the author, but to maintain an evenness of tone, at some points these have been lightly adapted. In the original French text, the scriptural references are given as footnotes, but they have been incorporated into the main text; generally, since French translations have their own flavor, the scriptures have been translated from the French rather than using some recognized English version.

One difficulty, since it is not clear from the French, has been when to capitalize the w in "word." We have felt it best to capitalize whenever it refers to Jesus, the Living Word, or to the Word of God, the Bible; when it refers to an individual word to a person it has not been capitalized. The French does not capitalize pronouns referring to God, and this practice has been followed in the translation.

Many thanks are due to Mrs. Hélène Hétu and all the people of the Bethasda Association who collaborated to make this work possible.

Roger Wilkinson

PREFACE

The pathways I intend to explore in this book took shape as a result of my personal experience. Little by little I came to understand the vital relationship there is between psychology and faith.

I come from a Catholic family, which, however, through my childhood and adolescence, was not a practicing one. When I was about nine and again at the age of fourteen, I took some important steps of faith: I had an encounter with Christ. From that time on the spiritual dimension seemed to be the only one that could provide meaning to my life, but I was totally ignorant as to the psychological level.

My career as a lawyer, which I pursued in Morocco, where I was born, occupied most of my time. It was the arena in which I endeavored to live my faith, inspired by the life of Ghandi, who, in the same profession, had taken a vow to act in accordance with truth, and whose political commitments were carried through in the spirit of the Beatitudes. I was part of a team which was active in favor of reconciliation between the Muslim, Jewish, and Christian communities that live alongside each other in Morocco. Later, I became committed with other believers to sharing a simple life and choosing non-violence; in this way I sought to integrate my faith into my life.

With the passing of the years I found myself in the midst of an internal crisis, with problems that prayer could not resolve. It was beyond understanding and brought me to despair.

During this time I was living in a small community in the far south of Morocco, and a doorway began to open. I confided in a priest who was passing through, telling him of my powerlessness to overcome a relationship blockage. He told me that it was useless to work at things on the basis of the symptoms, and that the epicentre of my difficulty lay elsewhere and that it was up to me to uncover it. This was an incredible encouragement to me: there was a way out, and I was not condemned to wander indefinitely. I became aware of an unexplored land within, and so began to discover the psychological dimension of my life. I underwent psychotherapy, but was so poorly equipped in my faith that for a time I put it on hold. The psychological arena seemed to me at that time to be the only secure ground.

Two years later a good, positive move brought me back in touch with Christian groups and I came to Chalon-sur-Sâone, to a seminar conducted by George and Victoria Hobson of the Episcopalian Church (the American branch of the Anglican Church). The theme was "inner healing." I was hearing this term for the first time and to me it seemed full of good sense, bringing a new direction to, and a lively, vital understanding of the word of God. In the course of the meeting I understood the articulation, the possible and necessary union, between the psychological and spiritual planes. Immediately I realized that I had arrived at port, that I had found what I had been seeking for many years; I still retain an enormous sense of thankfulness to George and Victoria, who opened up this way for me.

I then began my endeavor to live for myself what I had discovered. I enjoyed very deep exchanges with others who were walking the same path. The process of psychotherapy proved irreplaceable; it enabled me to get to know myself, to draw closer to the truth about myself, to bring into the light the knots I had tied in myself or had allowed to become established over the course of my life. This was the beginning of a great reestablishment of order and meaning.

Month by month, the psychological area fell into place and the spiritual was restored too. Every day my faith became more true, alive, deeply rooted and also more humble. However, at some points, particularly when it came to guilt, I remained bound, oppressed. Nevertheless I had a certainty that the word of Jesus which announces liberty to the captives had to be fulfilled in my life.

It was at this time that I discovered that the Holy Spirit is truly alive and at work in me, as he is in each human person, and that I had to learn to collaborate with him.

I had become aware that the psychological and physical planes needed to open onto the spiritual. The wrong paths I had taken had not only to be explored on the psychological level, but constituted transgressions of the fundamental laws of life, the laws of God which I had misconceived; I had been living according to entirely false notions about suffering, expiation, and reparation, and had been making God a God of condemnation. I saw my responsibility clearly and the choice I had either to be imprisoned in my past or find a pathway of life.

To adhere to the word of life meant that I had to change direction, to quit my destructive ways, to learn the ways of life that the word was showing me. In God's grace, I experienced that this was possible, and thus discovered what to do with all I had learned through psychotherapy.

The process never ends and some fragilities remain, but there is a source of deep peace because the way forward is clear; the word of God takes on fuller and fuller meaning, always accompanied by the power of the Spirit.

In 1987, Sister Minke, prioress of the community of the Sisters of Grandchamp in Switzerland (a monastic community of sisters from a Reformed background), asked me to give some teaching on the ways of inner healing, the evangelization of our depths. With this starting point, little by little, with the prayerful and vigorous participation of the Sisters of Grandchamp, we have developed an annual cycle of three sessions in which teaching, group sharing, individual mentoring, and personal time alternate. These cycles are now held in France and at Grandchamp, which remains the foundational place for our team as well as our prayer bulwark.

The courses are run by an ecumenical group in an association named Bethasda.[1] Together we reflect, pray, and work unceasingly, willing to spend and be spent.

I would like to express here my debt of gratitude to Marie-Madeleine Laurent, psychologist. It is thanks to her reflections, her experience, and her competence that I have been led to ponder the themes of human limitations, the drive to omnipotence, the burying of emotions, violence, the maternal and paternal functions of God's love, covetousness, and competitiveness.[2] I take up these different themes which we have developed in common, and, while holding to their key ideas, I develop them in my own way, according to my own specifics. Other clinical psychologists have joined our association, sharing their competencies with us. They have helped us not to "drift," but to head on in the right direction. The same is true when it comes to theology.

I also thank from the bottom of my heart all the men and women who have taken part in our sessions. The vigor with which they have begun,

1. Bethasda, Île-de-France, B.P.5292, 78175 Saint-Germain-en-Laye Cedex.
2. *Convoitise* and *rivalité*. *Convoitise* could also be translated as "envy."

their faithfulness, their friendship, the profound interest they have taken, all have been a great support to us, helping us to deepen our ability to serve; they are a constant source of renewal in our daily walk.

Since its first edition in 1997, this book has drawn together a great number of people on different continents. I receive an overflowing bag of mail from people bearing witness to the way the work has opened unsuspected, liberating horizons.

It is important never to forget that the disposition of the heart, which is the basis of everything, is a gift of God. Our part is to desire this gift and set ourselves in order.

I am asked what word I would have today for each person.

I leave everyone to seek a word for themselves, to ask for such a word. For myself, I would say just what Jesus says in John's Gospel: *"I will not leave you orphans. I will send you the Holy Spirit"* (John 14:18 and 15:26).

Simone Pacot
June 2015

INTRODUCTION

Have we been evangelized to the depths of our being and in every component facet? The question is whether the good news of Christ's message of life has reached into our deepest impulses, the most deeply buried and acute difficulties, our death wishes, our instincts of destruction and self-destruction. Are we really disposed to undergo this transformation, this implantation with a new life-force which will pull us out of death and into life, into renewed relationship with ourselves, with God, and with others, in the kingdom?

ARE WE STILL SICK BECAUSE OF OUR PASTS?

We are never passive with regard to our past, try as we may to repress it. Our past can't be changed, but it is certainly possible to change the consequences the past has in the present. The past can be a place of entrapment, of distress, of shame, or can become a springboard, the motor force for a life based on what we really are, and on what we have experienced. Very often an event in the present can reveal something of our failings. If a wound in our past has been dealt with badly, we are always liable to react disproportionately to the seriousness of the new event. We can be really deeply disturbed; there can be anger that rumbles or explodes, stubborn hatred, feelings of distress, of jealousy, of fear, of being frozen in relationship, the impression of being unable to escape, of being bound. Furthermore, we often repeat the same process in different forms: in fact, we keep reproducing the same maladaptive response in an effort to find a way out of our past; because we have no real idea of what the goal is we keep going round in circles. We can be separated from our freedom, our true identity lost or in abeyance, our emotional lives exaggeratedly dependent on others. Our personality can still be under the domination of "the other," mixed up in that person and unable to receive the love of God and to experience true love. All these conditions are symptoms, warning signs showing that we have not been truly evangelized in our depths.

What are we to do? In general we tend to pray to be healed of symptoms, but the deep problems remain. Then we think we lack faith and give way to discouragement and exhaustion. Sometimes it becomes necessary to undergo analysis or psychotherapy with a competent person (it is not a question under any circumstance of entrusting ourselves to risky, marginal[1] psychotherapies), but, evidently, this course of action should not be systematically applied to everyone. Many can experience very profound restoration as they awaken and come to peace through the discovery of fundamental points of reference that help them into their true standing as sons and daughters of God. As we come to a real understanding of God's word, of the great laws of life, as we learn to take proper care of the three elements of our being—the body, the soul or psyche (that is, our feelings, emotions, and affects . . .), and the spirit (the deep heart); as we set things in order, allowing the Spirit to breathe life into each part, and Christ to dwell there; and as we open ourselves and the whole of our past to the light of God, we will eventually leave behind our internal fragmentation and our lives will recover meaning. The way is simple and is open to all (Deut 30:11–14).

THERE IS NO MAGICAL HEALING

This journey of truth can only be walked in the company of mercy; its goal is an awakening to the areas of our lives that need conversion. We often long desperately for some kind of magic wand to be waved; we hope that the love of Christ will mean there is no need to go down unto the unspoken recesses of our bodies, our souls, our spirits, into an awareness of the false ways we have followed. We want healing but not necessarily conversion. This is the reason why, to me, it seems better to speak of the evangelization of the depths rather than healing.[2]

Nevertheless, God does really heal. He sets us free, at large, freeing us from our oppressions and bonds (Luke 4:18). He calls us out of our tombs (John 11:43–44). *Look! You are well,* Jesus the Christ said to the paralytic

1. Fr. *sauvages.* The reference is to high risk methodologies.
2. Or perhaps "inner healing."

by the pool of Bethesda (John 5:14). It is essential, though, to really understand the deep meaning of the healing that Christ proposes if we are not to fall by the wayside and remain on the periphery of our true selves.

Healing is often granted in a way that is very different to what we had expected. We so often long for a complete healing and then fail to appreciate the real restoration in which physical or psychological frailties remain. To accept and take these on board with a heart both brought to rest and illumined is real progress in healing. In the same way, we can often be looking for healing on some particular line when the reality is that another area is being touched and called to conversion. Renunciation of hope for immediate fruit is a fundamental attitude of heart; with it we become able to march onward, one foot in front of the other, day after day, learning obedience,[3] guided by the Spirit.

Generally speaking our concern is to be delivered from some specific trouble, some lesser thing that disturbs or disquiets us, from a troubling symptom—when in fact it is a manifestation of a much deeper pain. If the seed of life is received only in the intellect, mentally, if the Spirit and the word don't penetrate into the heart of all we are, deep into our flesh, deep into the internal turmoil, nothing is really touched. The way is one of incarnation, of the descent of the Spirit into our humanity, in full accord with the life of Jesus.

There is no reason for us to be anxious. The Spirit lives in us and he will help us to proceed. He it is who encourages us to follow this way of incarnation, the way of everyone who, at his or her own pace and through Christ, experiences the word becoming flesh (John 1:1–14), seeing what God says touch and affect us now.

GOD IS LOVE

The love of God is both paternal and maternal, as every love should be. The love of God is a true love. God is a father with the tenderness of a mother. He loves us in truth; his loving kindness takes joy in truth. Really it is preferable to talk about the paternal and maternal functions of God's love rather than of God as father and mother; nevertheless he is essentially, fundamentally, a father, meaning that his love is experienced without any confusion, at an appropriate distance—but he does still love us with the tenderness of a mother. Seeing God solely as a mother will always lead us

---

3. Literally "docility."

into the symbolism of fusional[4] love which does not allow the other person their separate existence.[5]

While God is infinite mercy, it is also he who gives us the great laws of life, laws that we cannot transgress without profound turmoil and unhappiness. The love of God is tender and merciful, but also luminous and full of life. It leads us to accept the truth about ourselves, and it would be unable to do otherwise because its concern is our freedom. Every good thing is provided by his grace and his mercy, but we are going to have our part to play.

On the evangelization pathway, then, the two fundaments are love and truth, each fully contained in the other; there can be no real love without truth, and there can be no constructive truth without love. It is because we encounter love that we become able to follow the road of return, to leave our blindness behind, to see ourselves as we are, and to accept being seen by God in the full light of day.

God is Love—he loves us with a merciful love, *agape* love. The love of God comes to us first, seeks us, and finds us. What good is there in wearing ourselves out in attempts to reach God when it is he who cannot get through and reach us, and is waiting for us to simply allow ourselves to be touched? He is always the one with the initiative. Henri Nouwen said exactly this: "Through much the greater part of my life I strove to find God, to know him, to love him [. . .] but now I ask myself if I have sufficiently realized that through all this time God has been endeavoring to find me, to know me, to love me . . ."[6]

Each of us is created and loved as a unique being. This is a fundamental law of life. Each of us has an identity that is entirely personal, with our own role and purpose to fulfill. This differentiation between us, this non-mixing of individuality, is an essential principle which is foundational to our relationship with God, to our identity, and to our future. It is our departure point, our anchorage, our reassurance; it is good news, our essential security. Each of us is welcomed as beloved (Matt 3:17),[7] called as a child (Luke 15:31), known by name (John 10:3), engraved on the palm of his hands. We are all of great price in his eyes (Isa 49:16; 43:4), regarded as very special. His love is given in its entirety, without comparisons, unmerited, without favoritism. Whatever our condition, our past, the form our

4. Fr. *fusionnel*. It might also be translated as "symbiotic."

5. Clément, *Athanase d'Alexandrie, sources*, 65.

6. Nouwen, *The Return of the Prodigal Son*.

7. French, *bien-aimé*, well-beloved.

sickness or path of death has taken, love is there, awaiting us; it knows no break, no interruption, and never quits, tenderly receiving and welcoming our weaknesses, our vulnerability, our sorrows and failures. We can open up to this kind of love; we can reveal everything about our pasts, without fear of being judged, rejected, or condemned. We are found, intently considered, and understood at the heart of our discouragement, exactly as was the invalid at Bethesda whom Jesus noticed in the middle of the crowd (John 5:6). We can weep, resting and leaning on the heart of the Father, allowing him to place his hands on our shoulders as we have the same overwhelming experience as the young man in the parable (Luke 15:20–24). The door of return to the Father is never closed, no matter how dirty or bedraggled, humiliated or ashamed, we might be, no matter how failing, confused, or exhausted. The Father is watching for us, he runs to meet us, takes us in his arms, embraces us, and celebrates, so great is his joy—even over just one person who returns to him. Allowing ourselves to be touched, wrapped up in, and restored by this love is the first step, the first foundational discovery.

However, the disordered nature of our love and the wounds to the heart that may have punctuated our pasts can persist as obstacles to our ability to receive the love of God. If we see love as unthinkable, beyond reach, dangerous and menacing, if we have taken the place of the Almighty in our lives, seeing ourselves as alone with nothing to rely on save our own strength and competency, then the love of God will be unable to reach us; while his love is always on offer, it is not something he imposes.

What happened for us to become unable to receive God's love? How are we to let ourselves be loved? This is a basic question, and one that we will be answering as we go.

GOD IS TRUTH

We find our reference points in him, as we learn the laws of life which enable us to reorientate correctly. Through his grace we enter an awareness of ourselves, allowing the light of truth to shine on us; we now have real choices and can abandon the ways of death for the way of life; we get back on track; we can rise and take up our bed through faith in his word, like the man at the pool of Bethesda (John 5:6–9).

Many people have made this wonderful discovery of the personal love of God, and have gone on to a true encounter. Their lives have been completely changed; there is a before and an after. However, there is a further possibility: without realizing it, we begin to say to ourselves that since God is love, there is nothing to do but simply receive. We present our wounds and problems to God, expecting him to do everything in our place, hoping in this way not to have to go through the process, the pathway of truth! We can forget that we are called to live in active collaboration with the Spirit and participate in the saving work of Christ within us. In a way, this means only receiving the maternal aspect of God's love, and so completely covering over and ignoring the way of return, the essential process that sees us going deep within to get ourselves back in order. There is a danger of regressing, becoming childish, on the pretext of recovering a childlike heart. God's love does not infantilize the human person; it requires us to stand upright, vibrant, throughout life's trials. Yes, God saves. He gives us the kingdom, but he calls us to be transformed, to move on from being his image and into his likeness, to fulfill our calling as sons and daughters of God as we engage with our freedom.

It is essential that we live in the fullness of these two aspects of God's love, to watch and not to fall into either of the traps that may ensnare us: to believe that God will do everything for us; or to rely on our own strength, forgetting that we are loved, longed for, and saved. In this latter case, we can become hardened, burnt out, depriving ourselves of God's gift, no longer knowing how to receive salvation. Instead of contemplating him, we dry out and wither.

In God's grace, through the paternal function of his love, the human person can recover his or her true bearings and be restructured through learning the great laws of life and adhering to them. We must live from his grace in order to develop our liberty, our identity; we are to become servants of the kingdom, each in our own specific task, and take up the spiritual battle that belongs to every son and daughter of God.

In the maternal function of God's love, in his womb of mercy,[8] we are to literally be reborn in love.

---

8. Fr. *Entrailles de miséricorde*. KJV uses "bowels of mercy" for this idea; however, in the French, where Mary is told "blessed is the fruit of your womb," the word used for womb in some versions is *entrailles*. Hence this translation.

INTRODUCTION

RELATION BETWEEN SPIRITUAL
AND PSYCHOLOGICAL LAWS

"Spiritual laws never oppose psychological laws. We can say rather that they assume them. However their focus is not the same, and the spiritual cannot be reduced to the psychological."[9] They are wider in scope and their goal is different. Spiritual law goes beyond psychological law and gives it direction, its goal, but it cannot do away with, extinguish, ignore, or deny the psychological function.

The first goal of spiritual law is to make us aware of our status as children of God, of our future as sons and daughters of God, of our basic liberty. It leads us into gifting, into spiritual warfare, but not into a contradiction or negation of our psychological or biological realities. Spiritual law will only ever unify things in us that are fragmented, dissociated.

HOW THE HUMAN PERSON IS CONSTITUTED

The human person has three component elements, the spirit or deep heart, the soul or psyche, and the body. We are spirit, psyche, and body; each element is of itself just one part, so we are not simply psyche or body, but neither are we simply spirit; the person is a union of the three elements.[10] Our task will be to rediscover this union, or unity, by experiencing each element in its fullness. The deep heart is the center of our being, our most intimate place, the very heart of the heart the Bible talks about; not the seat of our feelings, but the place we encounter God. The psyche is the emotions, the affectivity, the feelings, the intelligence, the imagination, all our faculties, our mode of relating to ourselves and others. The body is the whole physical, biological level. The body, the soul, and the spirit do not operate on the same level. They interpenetrate, but they do not fuse. It is essential not to confuse their individual functions, but to clearly distinguish them. But neither is there any division or opposition, no dissociation.

The whole process of evangelizing the depths can be seen as this search for unity. We need to live with an integrated self, with none of the three elements neglected, allowing the Spirit to work freely; it is his role to unify us. Just as there is in creation, there is in us an internal order which we need to know and respect.

9. Xavier Thévenot, in a personal note to the author.
10. Larchet, *Thérapeutique des maladies spirituelles.*

EVANGELIZING THE DEPTHS

THE GOAL OF THE PROCESS

What are we looking for as we set out in this direction? Total and immediate healing, perhaps? The suppression of the symptoms that so trouble us? Or perhaps for a form of happiness, of well-being, of self-fulfillment? None of these are our goal, and it is most important not to be mistaken about this. The goal of our endeavors to evangelize the depths is to give God his rightful place in our lives; it is to return to him in the fullness of our humanity, allowing our humanity to be animated by the Spirit. In this way we conform to God's salvation in every area of our beings, we are set in order as we are re-attuned to the fundamental laws of life. In this way we experience in its fullness our status as sons and daughters of God, servants of the kingdom.

The goal then is to live a "Passover," a movement of conversion, returning to God, and thereby realizing the reality of our baptism. We will go down into the waters of Jordan, into the midst of our past, and open up to life as we hear the words which are meant for us too—*This is my beloved Son* (Matt 3:17). The way begins with ourselves—since this is our first responsibility, our first field of activity—but it is not to finish with ourselves; we are the point of departure, but not the goal,[11] and we will see with wonderment that, as we walk towards conversion, the world around us will also begin to be renewed; we thus become true workers in the Lord's vineyard (Luke 10:2).

11. Buber, *Le Chemin de l'homme*, 42.

THE WORD OF GOD

The healing of the sick man at the pool of Bethesda

JOHN 5:1–18

¹ After this there was a feast of the Jews; and Jesus went up to Jerusalem.

² Now at Jerusalem by the sheep market there is a pool, which is called in Hebrew Bethesda, having five porches. ³ In these there lay a very large number of invalids, the blind, the lame, the paralyzed, waiting for the moving of the water. ⁴ For an angel went down at a certain time into the pool, and troubled the water: whoever stepped in first after the troubling of the water was made whole of whatever disease they had. ⁵ There was a certain man there, who had had an infirmity for thirty-eight years. ⁶ When Jesus saw him lying there, and knew that he had been like that for a long time, he said to him, "Do you want to be healed?" ⁷ The impotent man answered him, "Sir, I don't have anyone to put me in the pool when the water is troubled: but while I am coming, someone else steps down before me." ⁸ Jesus said to him, "Rise, take up your bed, and walk."[1] ⁹ Immediately the man was made whole, and took up his bed, and walked. It was the Sabbath day. ¹⁰ The Jews therefore said to the healed man, "It is the Sabbath: it is not lawful for you to carry your bed." ¹¹ He answered them, "The man who made me whole, he said to me, 'Take up your bed, and walk.'" ¹² Then they asked him, "Who is it that told you to take up your bed, and walk?" ¹³ And the healed man didn't know who it was since Jesus had conveyed himself away and there was a large crowd. ¹⁴ Afterwards Jesus found him in the temple, and said to him, "See, you have been made whole: sin no more, lest a

---

1. *Rise, take up your bed and walk.* "Être acteur de sa vie" ("Being the active party in your life") is the title of a working paper by Marie-Madeleine Laurent and Dominique de Bettignies, based on this Gospel passage.

worse thing come upon you." [15] The man went away, and told the Jews that it was Jesus who had made him whole. [16] Therefore the Jews persecuted Jesus, and sought to kill him, because he had done these things on the Sabbath day. [17] But Jesus answered them, "My Father is always at work, and I work." [18] For this reason the Jews sought to kill him all the more, because not only had he broken the Sabbath, but he also said that God was his Father, making himself equal with God.

When Jesus saw him lying there, and knew that he had been like that for a long time, he said to him, "Do you want to be healed?"

Jesus was in Jerusalem at the time of a Jewish feast, a Sabbath day, in a building equipped with a pool named Bethesda. Around the pool there was a *multitude . . . of the blind, lame, impotent,* all awaiting the moving of the water which indicated the passing by of the angel of the Lord; they would then rush forward and the first person in would be healed. Jesus was there, in the midst of all this agitation, and, as always, unstressed or overburdened, full of the presence of God, aware of everyone. He noticed a particular man lost among the crowd, unmoving and silent. The place is described in some detail, but no detail is provided about this man, which seems to indicate that he did not himself know too much about who he was. Jesus took the initiative in their meeting because it was a Sabbath day, but also very decidedly because the man was so lacking in life that he had neither the strength nor the courage to ask for help. He was completely passive. He was there, but in fact was making no effort at all, as so often happens when things are going wrong: we see no way out, we lose courage, we think everything is lost.

Jesus went up to him. The man was unable to move, so Jesus moved. It is God who loves first. He knows our deepest needs. He comes knocking at our door when we are broken. The grace of God comes to seek his lost children, to lead them back to his house.

Jesus interested himself in the man as though they were the only two there. He looked at him, spoke to him, questioned him, gave him his time, listened to his answer, and carefully waited until something within him began to move. In this way he brought a first and fundamental healing—he revealed that the man had value, that he was a person, that he counted as someone, that he was worthy of interest, that he was loved uniquely, as is every child of God.

Jesus said to him, "Do you want to be healed?"

With this one, penetrating question Jesus revealed to the man the cause of his sickness: he had allowed his vital forces to die, his desire to live, and he no longer knew how to want. Jesus looks beyond the outward appearance; he never concerns himself solely with the externals of the person; he has not come to heal the manifestations of some twist, some ill, but to heal the cause. "Jesus is there, the bearer of grace, which is to say the bearer of a God who comes to seek and set in motion the man's vitality and lead him to healing."[2]

"Sir," the infirm man replied, "I don't have anyone to put me in the pool when the water is troubled: but while I am coming, someone else steps down before me."

Jesus' question was direct and therefore called for a definite response, yes or no. No one could take the man's place; only he knew where he stood. Nonetheless, in his answer he spoke about others, not of what he was going through, wanted, or felt: *There is no one to put me in the pool*, to carry me. However, he understood the challenge. This means to us that whatever our state of distress, it is always possible to hear God's voice; it pierces our darkness, which is unable to block it (John 1:5).

The sick man responded. His reply was beside the point, but he did reply; he opened the channels of communication. This was enough: a drop of life began to flow, the healing process had begun as the man had made a move, a very small act, probably the only one he could make; now he was in relationship with the one who was pursuing him: in his own way he had opened the door.

Jesus said to him, "Rise, take up your bed, and walk." And immediately the man was made whole, and took up his bed, and walked.

Jesus had given the command to live. The man obeyed; he didn't know who Jesus was, but somehow knew he was the bearer of life. He could quite equally have stayed there on his bed. However, he clung to the resurrection. Jesus didn't touch him as he did with so many other sick people; neither

---

2. Pastor D. Marguerat, a teaching given during a retreat on the "chemins de guérison dans l'Évangile" ("paths of healing in the Gospel").

did he take him by the hand to help him get up, precisely because the man's healing was to take place through the man's recovered confidence in his identity. He had to choose to get up himself, to recover his desire to live.

Everything was given as a total gift; it is God who heals. He does however require of us an internal action to take hold of the gift. The action required of this man was to not close the door by thinking of himself as unworthy of God.

However, he did not leave his bed immediately. He was commanded to "take it up," not to throw it away. To pick up one's bed needs a definite decision. "To take up" is an active verb, whereas to be "lying down" is to be passive. To take up one's bed is to reverse things, change direction, replace a movement towards death with a movement into life. To take up and carry the bed instead of discarding it means that we are not starting out from scratch, but standing up and setting out with our past as the starting place. Taking up the bed means no longer being shackled to what is wrong. It is to be aware of our real problems, to leave victimhood behind; it is to no longer be waiting for others to carry us and put us in the pool.

We will all have our part to play as we carry our own bed. Then the day will come to be rid of it and, in God's grace, we will become able to "let go of that which has harmed us."[3]

Afterwards Jesus found him in the temple, and said to him, "Behold, you are made whole: sin no more, lest a worse thing come upon you."

Along the way the man again encountered Jesus, who continued his work of awakening. Of course, there was no threat in this. The man had welcomed God's gift. He was up and about, living instead of as good as dead. Only at this moment did Jesus impress his own responsibility on him. He was now able to understand what had happened to him, could look his sickness in the face and name it because he had met with living love. This is where we find the truth, the power of God's love as it admonishes us: "Do not take up your old habits, your old clothes; but watch, take care of the life that is newly born in you."

The normal—inevitable—relapses do not mean that something worse is happening. The "worse thing" would be to lie down again after a fall instead of taking the bed up again and recommitting to the way forward. It would also entail thinking that everything has already been done, when

---

3. Basset, *Le Pardon originel*, 422.

in fact it is indispensable to watch (Mark 13:33) and care for the life so that it bear fruit. In the end, it would be to cease to rely on grace and instead stagnate in powerlessness.

PART ONE

Opening Up to the Spirit

1

THE INVITATION

Take away the stone (John 11:39) said Jesus in front of Lazarus' tomb. Take away anything that prevents the breath of God from penetrating into your dead places. Open whatever in you is closed. Do away with your resistances. When Jesus wanted the stone over Lazarus' tomb removed, Martha was distraught: *Lord, he will already be stinking; it's been four days.* Jesus disregarded this; he had come to enter places that did not smell nice, to open what was locked, to heal what was sick, to return to life whatever was dead.

Behold, I stand at the door and knock; if anyone hears my voice and opens, I will come in and will dine with them, and they with me (Rev 3:20). The invitation is all tenderness, longing, and liberty. It leads us immediately into an internal movement. As always, it is God who takes the initiative. It is Christ and the Spirit who are knocking at the door. Christ seeks to be welcomed by the human person in the most special way, into a close relationship, one unexpected and previously unknown. The Spirit seeks entrance in order to create, to set right, to restore, and to unify. We must desire this entrance of the Spirit with our whole being, knowing, even if unable to put it in words, that there is a lack in us, an emptiness which is in fact the desire to know God, whatever name we may choose for him. There is a profound affinity between us and the Spirit. The Spirit is impatient to come in to fulfill his function, and our flesh is thirsty for him. Do we hear the knock at the door? Are we opening the door? Or are we merely at the edge of our selves, cut off from the source? Are we aware that God has his dwelling in the human person and that we are therefore the temple of the Spirit, and that we can literally live from the life of God, being fed and watered by it?

Ephatha (be opened) (Mark 7:34). This was a word from Jesus addressed to a man shut up in himself. He couldn't hear and only spoke with great difficulty, completely turned in on himself, on his malaise. Jesus put his fingers into his ears, spat and touched his tongue . . . and said to him, *"Ephatha," which is to say, Be opened. Immediately his ears opened and his tongue was loosed* (Mark 7:34–36).

WHAT IS THAT WE ARE TO OPEN?

The issue is to open to the Spirit the whole of our being, not just the heart or whatever aspect of ourselves seems right to us and with which we are most familiar. Our being as a whole is the treasure we have been entrusted with. It has a history, a depth, a reality, a potential for riches and resources we may never have tapped. The first step is to allow the Spirit to circulate freely through every area of our being, to bring fresh air, to ventilate, re-wire, bring new life, re-direct. This opening up necessarily leads us to a new awareness of the way we are habitually living. Often we have vacated some area of ourselves which therefore lives in exile, far removed from our internal source; in the end it is dying of hunger like the prodigal son (Luke 15:17), or withered like a branch cut off from the vine (John 15:6).

This dissociation can take many forms. Some people are very much at ease physically in their rapport with the ground, with material things, but they have lost the way of the heart, their sleeping heart. Others basically develop their minds and are no longer in touch with their emotions; these are not understood—the deep pains of hatred, anger, jealousy . . . never come to the surface. Many people only live at the emotional level, and are therefore liable to be taken over by disordered feelings and to wear themselves out in an unbalanced, misdirected search for love. Others, by contrast, anaesthetize themselves, barring the way to emotional expression; the emotional life can be frozen over following a lack or loss of love, some betrayal, or insecurity. Perhaps people decide not to love again rather than risk the pain of eventual break up and loss, and not let themselves be loved rather than risk betrayal and abandonment. Our sensitivity, this treasure with which we are entrusted, dries up. The body, perhaps, ceases to fulfill its proper function; it can become the sole concern, or, if as a child we were not held affectionately or were abused, it can become tense, locked down and defensive. To interest oneself solely in the spiritual, neglecting the physical and the psychological, is simply dangerous. It is really necessary to recover the unity of the body, the affective capacity, the sensibility, the emotions.

Opening up to the Spirit, to Christ, is not so easy. It is an internal movement which is not difficult in itself, but it comes up against the stone that blocks the entrance, against resistances that stem, most of the time, from not having dealt with our wounds in a healthy way. It is certainly not to be a source of disquiet if we find ourselves unable to open up all at once; in fact this is altogether normal. Our lives are surrounded, defended by chain mail! This is far from bad—it is good to be protected; but it is essential that little by little we leave behind mistrust of self and welcome the initial changes in ourselves as precious sources of information, to finally dare present ourselves to God just as we are, without fear, in full confidence.

THE OMNIPOTENCE OF GOD OR OMNIPOTENT LOVE?

We live in a world of so many power relationships. As victims of this we have to face up to our desire to be almighty. Quite naturally, we tend to represent God's omnipotence as a reflection of our human desire for the same power; this will certainly color our relationship or refusal to engage in relationship with God. It is essential not to open ourselves up indiscriminately—this can be dangerous indeed. "The idea of Power is ambiguous; power can bring great good to pass, but also do much harm."[1] To entrust oneself to an omnipotent God but without first examining this notion is simply dangerous since it is hard to know how to think of our own liberty in such a relationship. "To say that God is omnipotent is to give as a backdrop a power which can be exercised as domination and destruction."[2] It is a mistake to premise the almightiness of God and then tack on as an afterthought the statement that he is love. "The omnipotence of God is the omnipotence of love; it is love that is almighty."[3] We need to take hold of the fundamental difference there is between "an omnipotent being who loves us, and omnipotent love. In God there is no power other than the power of love."[4] We can open the door to this love without fear.

Together with love, light and truth will come in, and they work in the same way as Christ, which means completely safely: *"For the Father himself*

1. Varillon, *Joie de croire, joie de vivre*, 25.
2. Varillon, *Joie de croire, joie de vivre*, 25.
3. Varillon, *Joie de croire, joie de vivre*, 26
4. Varillon, *Joie de croire, joie de vivre*, 26.

loves you" (John 16:27). We will never be pulled down, compelled, savaged, or abandoned. However we must still be careful not to identify God's love with the merely emotional, with the sentiments. This is a common confusion which stems from the way in our languages the word "love" means several different things—though it does still best convey what we can glimpse of God's nature. In order to be more specific about love, the New Testament authors used the word *agape* ("charity"), signifying that God's love should not be confused with sentiment. The love of God is the source of all love, and he "trans-dynamizes,"[5] purifies, directs human love; our human love then keeps its physical and emotional characteristics even as it is called to express *agape*. That the love of God is not to be confused with human love does not mean that it is distant and abstract; no, it envelops, accompanies, and burns in our heart every moment of our lives. Often though, we are not really conscious of it, so we need to awaken to the constant, multiple manifestations of God's love in our lives, to his presence at work at every turn. We should be grateful instead of murmuring and complaining, entering into the goodness of just being.

5. Literally translating the French *transdynamiser*, which itself is a neologism from an oral teaching given by Xavier Thévenot.

2

THE OBSTACLES

THE FEAR OF GOD

You are not to make any idol, nothing that bears the image of anything in heaven, here on earth or in the waters under the earth. You are not to bow down to such gods, and you are not to serve them, for it is I who am the LORD your God (Deut 5:8–9).

This is one of the first teachings of the Bible. You are not to create a God in the image of your father or mother, of this or that representative or aspect of the church, of some authority. You are in no way obliged to engage with your God in a relationship of fear, rejection, or fusion such as might have been your experience with people; he is the Altogether Other. However, this is often our first and most fundamental idolatry. The idols of Deuteronomy are not simply physical forms, that is, external images of a visible nature, but are also the mental image that we form for ourselves of God. *The world has not known you* (John 17:25), Jesus said to his Father. Are we allowing Christ to reveal God to us? Do we allow God to reveal himself to us? Or do we place our own hand on revelation and create a God in our own image? Do we protect ourselves from God and mistrust him? The question merits whatever attention we pay it.

We will never be able to desire a life in God as long as we believe he is a rival to the human person and that his omnipotence is a threat. Under such conditions we think he will alienate our identity (that we will cease to exist, no longer have our own thoughts, will, or desire—that we will be devoured), our freedom (that we will be submitted to unbearable pressure), our very life (that God will take no account of our limitations and that we will be overrun by a life that will crush us). How often we think that he punishes, accuses, condemns, oppresses; that he is the source of evil and suffering, that he desires our death, not our life.

In what ways do we reduce God and
recreate him in our own image?

A great part of our trouble is that we create an image of God based on the people to whom we first relate. A young child can hardly do other than transpose onto God the picture that they have of their father, their mother, their other relatives and their teachers. Without being aware of it, we settle with God the accounts we have with our parents!

You are my beloved Son (Mark 1:11).

> Jesus understood these words as the deep truth of his being. The power sustaining him in the moment was not the love of a man for God, but the very love of God for man, for all humanity. In him, God drew near in a way that is completely new and beyond compare. This is the good news it was his mission to announce.[1]

Unfortunately we nearly always project onto this word "Father" what we know about our own fathers or mothers. The wounded child reacts, rebels, and believes that no one will ever be interested in him or her because they simply aren't worth it; this child is unable to imagine a relationship with a father or mother that is free, vibrant, warm, and real. He, she becomes fixed into the idea that this new world to which they are such a stranger simply doesn't exist and so closes the door to such a gift.

So for some, love is dangerous. To those who have known a love that seeks to merge possessively and so oppresses, love is experienced as a threat.

Joël was a person who distrusted love. If he was to open the door he would be devoured; God would invade and take possession of the one place that belonged to him. He had to disconnect his image of God from that of a parent who had loved him misguidedly, rejecting the false idea of a person who would steal his very being.[2]

---

1. Leclerc, *Le Royaume caché* (The hidden kingdom), 81.
2. Sibony, *Pour une éthique de l'être* (Towards an ethics of being), 340.

Michel had a father who was extremely authoritarian. He had no idea of the liberty of a child of God and was unable to picture it; the least act of freedom seemed to him to be a transgression and he immediately felt guilty. He lived out a false sense of submission to his erroneous conception of God's law, the true nature of which he had not internalized.

Anne had known only a conditional love—you will be loved if you correspond to my desires, if you fulfill your role as the older child. She could not imagine being loved freely for what she was. She lived with the fear of being rejected if she failed to meet the expectation of "the other." She had no capacity to receive from God the love he gives us freely: she had to merit love.

Healing calls us to return to the parental or sibling relationships, becoming aware of the way any wounds may have been infected. Then only is it possible to recognize that God is different from our father or mother, to renounce false ideas and then allow space to receive what God is saying.

We often construct the image of God that we need in order to meet our emotional lack or to reassure ourselves with a misplaced sense of security. How easy it would be if God literally replaced the father or mother who was missing, if he brought a spiritual feeling that compensated for the absent tenderness, or a form of love that would eliminate suffering, would make us invulnerable, make our exercise of choice unnecessary, and remove all need to take any risk—and would surely heal us, and in the way we wish!

"God, the source of suffering and evil?"[3]

To hold God responsible for suffering and evil is to participate in the most erroneous of ideas, but one frequently advanced, often unwittingly. Yes, evil and suffering are there; they will assail us and inevitably we ask questions. It is not unusual, then, to think that God wishes our suffering, the sacrifice of our lives, and death.

Evil has two forms, suffering and sin. God wants neither of them and is the origin of neither of them. Suffering and evil are part of this world so marked by transgression. Suffering is inherent to the human condition and comes from ourselves, from others, from the world, but never from God. It forms part of our limitations and can attack our body, our psyche, our spiritual life, our social life. On no account should we seek it; rather we are to protect ourselves from useless suffering—and not be complicit in our

3. Thévenot, *Souffrance, bonheur, éthique*, 31.

own eventual destruction. Jesus in no way colluded with suffering. At no point in his earthly life do we see him send suffering on anyone. "For him suffering was not an ally but an enemy."[4] He didn't give any explanation for evil and did not really reply to the "why" we all pose. He shows us how to face suffering when it is unavoidable, and that indeed, as we take on board the grace and presence of God, it becomes a stage on the way to maturity and leads to life, to Paschal life.

The cross

If we have false ideas about the cross, about the will of God, atonement, about reparation, this will bring fundamental disorders at every level. How many of us believe that God wished the death of Jesus to pay for our sins, and have therefore simply adopted the unacceptable idea of human sacrifice! The will of God, to which Jesus clung with his whole being, conforming to his central desire, was not that he be tortured and executed on a cross, but that he completely fulfill his mission of incarnation.

At no moment of his life did Jesus seek suffering. He lived in full accordance with his purpose, announcing what he had to announce, without sweetening anything. Love and light streamed out wherever he went as the kingdom came near to the little ones. However, from month to month the violence of the Pharisees became more and more menacing and his message collided full on with the violent religious structure. He fled the persecution when he could, but eventually found himself faced with the inevitable outcome, a trial and a death sentence. This was a result he would have loved to avoid, but he faced it and chose to pursue his allotted task to the end. He denied nothing of all he had to accomplish. He refused to respond to violence with violence; love would not permit it. He brought to light a new consciousness by non-violent means. "For Christ, to obey the Father was not to carry out an order in the way we would see an inferior carrying out an order from the hierarchy. We must not imagine God the Father as saying to God the Son: 'I order you to suffer and to die at thirty-three.' If that is obedience, we would have to agree with anyone who might protest and refuse it!"[5]

---

4. Thévenot, *Souffrance, bonheur, éthique*, 31.

5. Varillon, *Joie de croire, joie de vivre*, 75.

We can say that "God the Father is on the same side as Jesus"[6]—against foolishness, intolerance, hunger for power, and blindness. He was to accompany him through the tragic hours that followed. God's will is manifest in the way Jesus approached the great drama, not in the fact of the event itself, as though God willed it. This was Jesus' obedience, to live through an event which was not of God's doing, as a son of God, as a son of light, in an intimate connection with his Father, as had been his constant way of life throughout his ministry since its springtime in Galilee. He would encounter a dark night, a desert, but his connection with the Father never slackened.

To live through all that happened as a son of God does not mean that he did so as some kind of superman freed from human constraints and earthly contingencies. We see him behaving as a sensitive, vulnerable, human person under attack. He experienced intense internal and physical pain, he met with betrayal, lies, and loneliness (Luke 22:32–48). "He was not spared the experience of feeling that things did not make sense, of confusion of mind and panic. He did not evade his internal questionings."[7] He cried out, *My God, my God, why have you forsaken me?* (Mark 15:34). Never, though, did he allow any rebellion to take up residence in him during the dark night of Gethsemane. As he confronted his anguish and the extremes of solitude, he sought out the help of his closest friends—though he found them asleep. He experienced being torn between solitary prayer and the need for support.[8] At this point he longed to be freed of a trial which he had previously foreseen and accepted. He seems not to have been able to feel the presence of the Father which had before been so natural to him. He then understood that he had to face the future alone and ceased to resist, taking a leap of faith: *Not my will but yours be done* (Mark 14:36). In accordance with your wishes—this is the way I will act throughout.

From this moment on Jesus was totally at one with himself and was able to face the whole testing in God's strength. *Get up! We must go! The one who hands me over is here* (Mark 14:42). Jesus would die as the son of God, giving full personal attention to all those around him, including his torturers, for whom he sought pardon, centered on love and on his Father. Everything demonstrates that deep in his heart, with pure faith, in the empty place within, he remained one with the Father. He was not a passive

---

6. Joseph Pyronnet in an oral teaching.

7. Thévenot, *Compter sur Dieu*, 137–40.

8. Hétu, *Quelle foi?* 212–14.

victim, and there is no question of mere resignation. Make no mistake, he said, my life *is not taken away from me, but I myself give it* (John 10:18). He transformed what might have been an unbearable constraint, a catastrophe, into a gift; there is therefore no unreason in what happened, and out of death there sprang a seed of life. In this way he teaches us how to choose to live as a child of light in circumstances we would never have chosen but are imposed upon us,[9] how to bear our cross instead of being subjected to it (Matt 16:24), how to take up our bed instead of just lying there, how not to be locked in by a situation but to bring meaning to events that in themselves have none, how to get back on track in life. We can discover an overall meaning to our lives, and yet we are often faced with events that seem scandalous and void of reason. Jesus teaches us to transform "looking for meaning" into "giving meaning," which is to say, "becoming once again the author, though not the sole master, of your personal history."[10] Christ shows us that life can gush forth from every situation; this is the meaning of Easter.

Similarly, "to affirm that Christ paid for us with his wounds" (Isa 53:5) or with his suffering is a shorthand replete with possible dangers, notably that of "believing that it is the suffering itself which redeems."[11] Suffering in itself is not redemptive; it is *love* that redeems. It is the way we behave during an event that makes it either a tomb or a doorway. We can experience it as a child of God or as an orphan, an unfortunate. It is the life of Jesus as a whole which saves us—his birth, his daily life in Nazareth, the joys and pains of his public mission, his condemnation and death, his resurrection. He saves us by the way he took on and traversed his life as a son of God: at every moment of his life he remained present to the love of the Father, filled with the Spirit, open, loving, full of strength and vigor, even in his death.

"The spiritual cliché of 'offering up your sufferings' also needs to be subject to clarification."[12] There is no need to give thanks to God for misfortune, for sickness, for some cruel grief—all things that do not come from God. Through the evil, however, we can praise God, that is, hold on to the certainty that he is at work at the very heart of death, that a tiny seed of life will mysteriously, little by little, bud; and that life will forge a way, that a new Paschal dawn will succeed. All these false ideas about redemption and

---

9. This outline in no way proposes an exhaustive theology of salvation in Christ.

10. Thévenot, *Souffrance, bonheur, éthique*, 29.

11. Thévenot, *Souffrance, bonheur, éthique*, 26.

12. Thévenot, *Souffrance, bonheur, éthique*, 27.

expiation can lead us to self-destruction, and they are all the more danger-ous in that they are hidden behind a set-up we believe to be spiritual.

Perversion of the word

On the basis of these false notions of God we pervert the word, attributing to God the idea that he intends death, calling evil things that are good, and good things that are evil (Isa 5:20). The word impels us towards life, even when it is demanding and vigorous, when it requires us to quit the things we are addicted to and that harm us. It reconnects us and does not divide. When it directs us to separate ourselves from things, it is so that we can love better in a more grounded way. It clears up our contradictions. It cannot lead to psychological death, to the destruction of our health or bodies. It is exactly by a manipulation and perversion of the word that Satan tempted Jesus (Luke 4:1–13), and Jesus vigorously reproached the Pharisees for their endeavors in the same direction.

Woe to you Jerusalem, you who are unclean (Jer 13:27).

See, I set before you today life and blessing, death and adversity. . . . If you will not listen, I declare to you today that you will surely perish, you will not prolong your days in the land you are going into to possess when you cross the Jordan. Therefore, choose life that you may live, you and your descendants (Deut 30:15–19). We think that God curses and punishes; but God does not do so; it is we who draw adversity upon ourselves. The word warns, alerts; if we continue in chaos and confusion, if we ignore valid, true instructions, we will make ourselves unhappy: how unhappy you will be if . . . .

If a grain of wheat falls into the ground but does not die, it remains alone, but if it dies it will bear fruit in abundance (John 12:24). This for-mulation is not just a poetical image; Jesus is referring us to an essential law. To be fruitful we have to pass through a form of death. The problem is that there is a confusion between death and destruction; we don't know what it is we are to die to. We must not be mistaken about which death we have to go through. A false interpretation of the word can mean putting to death what ought to be alive in us, and allowing what ought to die, things that impede us, to live and prosper. "Jesus described and contrasted two dynamics of life. When life throws us off balance, we can react by hardening ourselves, shutting ourselves off, refusing to be subject to ill, and we do this by denying the experience. This way of responding amounts to a refusal to die, the desire to remain alone and sterile, according to Jesus' words. Faced with this kind of experience, we can, however, also consent to die, which is to say, open ourselves like the grain of wheat which accepts being in communion with the earth which receives it."[13] The evangelization of the depths is a way of living similar to the grain of wheat which falls into the earth and accepts the loss of its form. It is a way of dying to ourselves so that the seed can bear the fruit of life.

Whoever seeks to save their life will lose it, and whoever loses their life for my sake will save it (Matt 10:39). To lose your life: these words when misunderstood can lead to a pathway of death. How many people deny themselves the right to live, or throw themselves into frenetic activity with the idea that it is good to lose one's life—and finish completely dried up? "To guard your life is to continue to barricade your door, put on your armor, seal yourself into the works of man, refuse to allow yourself to be touched."[14] To lose one's life means first of all accepting that we receive our being from God, consenting to the idea that one's own life is not defined uniquely and solely by oneself. It is to consent to collaborate with the Spirit, to allow him to move and work freely within, to enter into this experience flexibly, to become oneself and be able to enter into true relationship as a true gift and so become servants of the kingdom.

If anyone will come after me, let him renounce himself, take up his cross and follow me (Matt 16:24). To take up the cross is a decidedly active, conscious affair. It is the reverse of passivity and resignation. It does not mean inventing crosses, false sacrifices, or taking another's cross upon yourself. It does mean assuming fully the burden of our own lives; it is to traverse the dangers and sorrows of life with Christ.

How do we leave behind false ideas of God?

Seek and you will find; knock and it shall be opened to you, Jesus tells us; *whoever seeks finds* (Matt 7:7–8). First of all, we need to take time to dust off our faith by studying simple, clear books on theology that will help us leave our haziness behind. We need to listen to the word, contemplating the life of Christ with a new outlook and an open heart, allowing the Spirit to guide us, teach us, and lead us into revelation.

Of course it is essential to become fully aware of our false ideas about God, to take careful note of them and look at them in the Spirit so that we

13. Hétu, *Quelle foi?* 269.
14. Hétu, *Quelle foi?* 268–69.

can see what wounds lie behind them and have produced them; and to become aware of the disconnect between what we say we believe and what we really believe at core.[15] Right here, for many of us, there is a real spiritual struggle. *You shall know the truth*, said Jesus, *and it will set you free* (John 8:32).

FEAR OF SELF

It is normal, that is, true for everyone, that we have limitations. Like Adam and Eve, however, we fall into the trap of refusing to acknowledge them (Gen 3:1–24). How we would love to be like God, to be God! This basic temptation, this rejection of our limitations, is found at the core of every human person, but it was conquered by Jesus during his forty days of fasting in the wilderness. It is highly significant that Jesus' temptations were concerned precisely with the accepting of human limitations and the rejection of omnipotence. Out of fear of seeing ourselves as we are, we hide from ourselves, and this leads us to fear being seen by others: *I was afraid because I was naked, so I hid myself*, Adam replied to the Eternal One when asked, *Where are you?* (Gen 3:9–10)—this was not geographical location; the meaning is "where are you *in yourself?*" Acceptance of our limits is a very deep conversion, an essential change.

Knowing oneself

The man and the woman were created in the image and likeness of God. This fundamental, ontological truth is revealed in the first lines of the Bible (Gen 1:26). The image of God is written deep into every human person; it is something given and indelible. The likeness of God is acquired. It is the goal and meaning of human life, growth into our condition as a son or daughter of God, each of us in a specific, unique form.

We are created and so loved as both flesh and spirit, loved both in the finite, visible form and also in our essence, that which is not finite and is invisible. Created as flesh, we are confronted by limitations of time and space, by weights and trials, by failures, errors, setbacks, by our constant falling, by limitations of gender . . . .

15. Thérèse Glardon, Bernard André, Jean-Claude Schwab in discussion with Hans Bürki, *Le Temps pour vivre*, 28.

Moreover, each person is sure to collide with their own specific personal limitations, their intelligence, their weaknesses, their past, their family; and again with the reality of others, differences that can be experienced as threatening, as opposition or indeed as complementary; in short, we confront factual reality.

We live from God, receiving the Spirit. Nevertheless, as we seek to live by the Spirit, how are we not to dream about going beyond our human condition? But this was not the way of Christ. He shows how to live as sons and daughters of God, taking on and integrating human limitations. This is our problem, and, at the same time, our normal condition. If tied to the earth, we become material. If we believe ourselves to be purely spirit, we settle into a form of flight from or rebellion from reality. In either case we are not whole. Our need is to live between these two poles and adjust and unify them. To live the infinite in the midst of the finite, to allow the Spirit to live in our flesh, this is the meaning of incarnation.

What does it mean to recognize our limits?

We mustn't blame ourselves for being limited. To do so would be as if we were to want forgiveness for being created finite. We firstly need to discern our limitations and name them. Only in this way can we accept them and take them on board; as we do so we become more at ease and cease to believe ourselves unworthy of being loved as we are. Our outlook changes on this basis and we understand that it is normal to have to face opposition, crises, difficulties. As there is less fear of self, of others, of God, we come closer to our true selves, and this sets us free. This self-acceptance is not resignation; resignation is a deadly form of passivity, and clean contrary to spiritual dynamics—no, this is a conscious, determined action, a choice which consists above all in ridding ourselves of illusions about ourselves, others, and our circumstances.

Renouncing the illusory is painful, a wrench; it entails a detachment from something deeply fixed in us. The first falsehood we have to renounce is the idealized image of ourselves we have created, the image which, instead of being true to ourselves, we pursue and have no desire to lose. It is difficult to be confronted by our imperfections, mistakes, and failings. It is so difficult to simply be ourselves; we want to be or have something other than what we are. The pagan conception of God is that to be loved by him we have to be perfect, which we often translate as meaning without failings or limitations; how often this leads to perfectionism. The following words of Jesus need to be understood in context: *You then are to be perfect as your heavenly Father is perfect* (Matt 5:48). They follow immediately after Jesus' invitation, *But I say to you, love your enemies, pray for those who persecute you, so that you may be truly children of your Father in heaven; he causes the sun to rise on the wicked and on the good, and the rain to fall on the just and the unjust* (Matt 5:44–45). The perfection Jesus is talking about does not mean being without limitations, but as Luke transmits it, is simply to love our enemies, to do good, and to lend without looking for anything back; then we will be children of the Most High (Luke 6:35).

In the same way, how often we pursue the dream of a perfect family, a perfect marriage, a community, rejecting a wounded and bruised world, a terrible relationship, love that is imperfect. The risk is that we become imprisoned in an ideal we have established for ourselves. This is a dream of omnipotence.

Accepting our limitations means learning from Christ how to live through disappointment, how to get back on track following betrayal, abandonment, or setbacks, how to live with a weakness or handicap. Disappointment can be terrible and we may become bitter, frustrated, and unable to regain trust; it can also be an occasion for deepening and maturing. As we accept that it forms part of life, it can become a dynamic, creative opportunity. This is what the disciples on the road to Emmaus experienced after Jesus' death as they recovered the sense of the presence of God at work in everything, including death (Luke 24:13–35).

To clarify, we need to question ourselves as to the limits we have not accepted, the grief we have not resolved, the denials into which we are locked. From the moment we begin to be aware of our limitations and finally accept them, it is as though we have reached our destination.

Freed of a great weight, we can stop tormenting ourselves. We become happy to have found ourselves, to be loved within the confines of our limitations, and to be back on route on the basis of what we are and not what we dream of being. This is healing, the first conversion, the truest act of humility there is.

Omnipotence

The logical and normal consequence of denying our limitations is the endeavor to be omnipotent.[16] The forms this takes are very insidious and it is often extremely difficult to recognize them. The moment we engage in any form of this power-assuming behavior, we have neither ourselves nor God in the right place, which is why this issue is central to the pathway of life. The relationship with God is the first thing that is directly affected, but the repercussions soon make themselves felt in our relationship with others. According God his rightful place and finding our own has a name—humility (Matt 11:29). Conversion leads us to humility, a word that comes from humus, soil; just like the earth, we receive everything from God. However, we so often have completely false ideas about humility. Humility does not consist in trying to compare our value with that of others and finding ourselves inferior or in self-deprecation, but in giving God his just place in our lives, knowing that everything comes from him, and that everything will be mere fallow ground without our co-operation with the Spirit.

There are two ways in which we endeavor to be all-powerful: firstly by ignoring God, and then by making ourselves out to be God. It is easy to understand what it would mean to ignore God, but to take oneself for God would be a much more ambiguous way to live, one which can be camouflaged behind an appearance of perfection, or of helping others.

We do without God essentially by depriving ourselves of his gifts. At times, we do this under the color of false humility, considering ourselves unable to be loved as we are, in our current state. "I am unworthy; how could God be interested in me?" We try to manage life on our own, as though cast into an empty universe and abandoned to our fate, totally failing to understand that we are literally and truly children of God. Again, we ignore ways to collaborate with the Spirit or live by the grace given us when we need help. We put a person or a thing or circumstance in God's place. We think that we will never make it. We live as though it is all or nothing: since we can't do everything, we do nothing. We become the proprietors of our own lives, our own gifts, our own projects, instead of allowing ourselves to be in-breathed by the Spirit and receiving from God.

We take ourselves for God basically by refusing to accept that anything escape our grasp; wanting to be the master of every situation and person; refusing to face our limitations and take our needs, fragility, and troubles

16. Gen 3:1–24, Thévenot, *Les Péchés, que peut-on en dire?* 29–31.

into account so that mistakes, fumblings, setbacks, falls, become unacceptable; by pursuing perfection in the sense of infallibility. We say that we have the truth, and refuse to entertain any form of questioning.

Omnipotence, the drive for power, can insinuate itself into the way we wish to help others. For example, we demand that they change in line with our views and take the path we think to be right for them. We seek to create their well-being in line with our idea of it, trying to ensure they don't suffer, and endeavoring to fill their every need. It can also exercise its influence on the spiritual level. We try to put our hand on God, to influence him with our claims and manipulate his word to make it serve our interests. We overturn his plans by tying ourselves up with vows and promises, taking a route that is not properly ours. Magic is introduced into our faith, and we short-circuit normal methods—work, the social sciences, medicine . . . . Finally, we see this desire for omnipotence in various forms of manipulating groups, or, more simply, people.

How we need to plead for grace to be alert to this trap, this all too common snare!

3

HOW DO WE OPEN THE DOOR?

This inner action does not involve making requests or supplications but is a response to an invitation; our place is to open up.

HEAR AND THEN OPEN

To hear and to open are two precise actions that require awareness, persistence, and collaboration, and are to be undertaken as we seek and welcome grace. To hear the invitation is in itself grace, and by his invitation Christ assures us that if we count on him then we can indeed open up. The reality is that the Spirit is already within us; it is inside us that he knocks, and we have simply to recognize this, that is, become aware that he is there, waiting.

We should not enter into endless reflections about how the opening of self will occur; faith is revealed and developed along the way as we walk, step by step, not just as a process of reasoning. When we don't know the Spirit well, we can simply ask him to manifest himself. It is enough just to set out by giving him a chance to do what he does; this immediately gives him a free hand.

Opening means removing the bars from what was shut up, taking away the stone rolled across the entrance. Opening is the reverse of folding in on oneself, of protecting oneself in an excessive way, of wishing to resolve the problems on our own or deny them, to stay at the edges. To open is to make a pact with the light.[1] It is a movement of life, an unfolding of what

1. Lafrance, *Persévérants dans la prière*, 78.

was folded, the beginning of healing. It means an end to stewing in our problems and allowing light and love to penetrate and a life-giving wind to blow. It doesn't mean shuffling a problem off with the unconfessed desire of ridding ourselves of it, pushing it away and so avoid facing it rather than take up our bed, carry it, and so accept our reality. We are active participants in the process; we open the door and enter with Christ into the heart of our difficulties, deep into each area of our selves, but enveloped, sustained, and strengthened by the presence of God, God who comes down into this precise place. We learn to go with him to the end of our suffering, our rebellion, our grasping for power, or our capitulation.

The Word became flesh (John 1:14). *He came to his own and his own did not receive him* (John 1:11). God's presence is not static but essentially dynamic; it is "efficacious, which is to say it necessarily changes whatever it touches . . . and this change is always in the sense of creation, re-creation, healing."[2]

If we are to understand what the presence of God produces in us, we need to think of "the influence of one who loves on the person loved. This influence works good, it transforms and comforts, strengthens, consoles, and sustains."[3] Opening means returning our keys to Christ, letting go our precious hold on the keys to our conscious and unconscious minds. This means the key to every door, those we have closed, perhaps unwittingly; the keys to every area of ourselves, the light and the dark, the fragrant and the less so. We must open up our wounds and traumatic memories and allow Christ to enter into the empty places of which we perhaps have no memory.

If anyone opens, I will come in . . . (Rev 3:20). From the outset we know that we are respected: Christ will never force the door but awaits our response. When our resistance ends he will enter . . . but he continues to knock. We are not risking anything; he is the shepherd who has come in search of his sheep and watches over them, those who have been treated harshly and stray in every direction, those for whom no one cares (Ezek 34:1–16). If our desire is clear and our choice is from our deep heart, the center of our will, Christ will enter through the closed doors (John 20:19), and the stone will be rolled away (John 11:39). The Eternal One said to Cyrus, "*I myself will go before you . . . I will shatter the doors of bronze and will break the bars of iron* (Isa 45:2). There is no irredeemably fixed situation; all things are possible to him.

---

2. An article by Father Vincent Thérien: "Nous avons vu la gloire de Dieu."

3. Thérien, "Nous avons vu la gloire de Dieu."

At times we can only begin opening up, and do no more than hold the door ajar, but this matters little—the important thing is to have taken the step. Any little fissure can be the point of departure for a complete turn-around: "I can't do everything, but the little I can do, I will." If we run into stubborn resistance on some point—"I can open up about anything except this"—we need to question ourselves: what are we protecting and why? We have to dwell on this precise issue. It may also be that we are just totally re-sistant, in which case we must ask the Spirit to make clear to us the reasons for our rejection. If our heart is humble and obedient, there is no doubt that the cause of the barrier will become evident.

Veronique was a person who took part in a healing session and expe-rienced an intense fear, a real sense of panic from the moment she heard this idea of opening up to God. She became aware that she couldn't, but also that she didn't wish to. Her life was one of giving, of welcome, of listening to others, but she realized that within herself there was an impossibility of sorts of opening up to others; she gave, but she never asked, and never received. During a counseling session she realized that when she was seven she had closed the door in a way that down to the present time was irrevocable and definitive. Faced with devouring, possessive parents, she had taken an un-shakeable decision—"you will not own me"—and this had evidently meant, "no one will own me, not even God." She therefore understood why she had been unable to open the door; but she could now recover this tiny corner of her past and find a way out different to the one she had taken. It was now possible for her to open to the One who was knocking, the One she had served for so long but without truly being able to give her heart.

In God's grace, everyone can take a step, at their own pace, to their own rhythm, and this is the step Christ calls us to—to allow the presence of God to live within, to permit the Spirit to inspire, fertilize, disinfect our human experience, so that the One to whom the earth and everything in it belongs might be present in everything (Ps 23:1).

SOME NOTES ABOUT THE WAY

The Spirit

When the Spirit of truth comes, *he will give you access to the whole truth* (John 16:13). This Spirit we speak about, who accompanies and leads us along the way, is the Spirit who lived in Jesus Christ, whom Jesus promised at the time of his departing. We no longer see Jesus in the flesh, but he announced that he would not leave us orphans, and that, in response to his prayer, the Father would give us *another Comforter, who will be with you always . . . the Spirit of truth* (John 14:18). Christ lives in us mysteriously by the Spirit, (John 14:16–17) and it is essential that we awaken to this spiritual reality. *Don't put faith in every spirit but test the spirits to see if they are of God because many false prophets have gone out into the world. This is how you will recognize the Spirit of God: every spirit that confesses that Jesus Christ has come in the flesh is of God* (1 John 4:1–2).

"The Spirit is the secret God, the interior God, deeper than our deepest depth."[4] Essentially it is the function of the Holy Spirit, who is given us by the Father, to help us pursue this immersion, into the shadows as well as the light, into the very heart of our being. He will take charge of us, but on the condition that we desire him, call upon him, recognize him, welcome him, and permit him to fulfill his function. It is essential that we learn to have a "true collaboration"[5] with him.

To live in, through, and from the Spirit right to the depths of ourselves is an experience that will depend on us—because he is always ready to go to work. Unhappily, passivity as a result of ignorance, inertia, or inattention is something that lies around the corner. The first act of setting our feet on the way, the first step, is to place total confidence in the wisdom and power of the Spirit; that is, we abandon the form of healing we had anticipated, ceasing to be fixated on some precise outcome and give our full agreement to him working freely.

Jesus, the Christ

He is at the heart of our journey. It is through him, with him, and in him that we are to walk. He is the way, the truth, the life (John 14:6). He is the true Son; he is so by nature, the only human being to have both a human nature and a divine nature. Jesus was born. He entered into flesh. This event of his incarnation is foundational, "the fruit of a long history, a lengthy, physical, worldly process."[6] Human sin transformed this event into the tragedy of redemption, but it remains above all the fulfillment of God's original design, "the grand synthesis in Christ of the divine, the human, and the cosmic."[7]

4. Clément, *Athanase d'Alexandrie, sources*, 68.

5. Leanne Payne, from *The Healing Presence*.

6. Clément, *Athanase d'Alexandrie, sources*, 39.

7. Clément, *Athanase d'Alexandrie, sources*, 38.

The birth of Jesus is the source of salvation, of the hidden recreation and reintegration of our beings. Through him our humanity can now be inhabited by the Spirit, brought to life in our deepest places. This is "our Easter, the movement of creation into the Kingdom of life."[8] "The Word was made the bearer of the flesh so that we might become the bearers of the Spirit."[9] We, through him, by adoption, can become sons and daughters of God. While it is by the Spirit that we are transformed into sons and daughters, clearly this is in Christ:[10] *Anyone who has seen me has seen the Father* (John 14:9). Jesus died, murdered, the innocent one who is living love, the light of the world. His life was ended by crucifixion because of his solidarity with humanity: "He took upon himself all the hatred, rebellion, derision, and despair."[11] He transformed the murder into a gift by offering his life, forgiving everyone, those who betrayed and abandoned him, and even his torturers.

"Henceforth for humanity there was no longer a question of any fear of judgment or of earning salvation, but instead, of welcoming love in trust and humility."[12] Jesus rose: "the victory over death is the victory over biological death, transformed in the process into a tremendous resurrection dynamic."[13] It is also "victory over spiritual death," over every internal death, "into which, abandoned to ourselves, we risk being shut forever."[14] Jesus has a unique and specific role, central to the restoration of the human person. He is not just a witness; salvation, deliverance, and transformation are mediated through him.

The deep heart

Hebrew language sees the heart as the inner being in a much larger way than do we, who tend to see the heart as the emotional life. In the concrete, inclusive anthropology of the Bible, the human heart is the real source of

8. Clément, *Athanase d'Alexandrie, sources*, 43.

9. Clément, *Athanase d'Alexandrie, sources*, 53.

10. Clément, *Athanase d'Alexandrie, sources*, 68. The expression "become sons and daughters of God," often used in this book, is always to be understood in this sense (see Rom 8:15).

11. Clément, *Athanase d'Alexandrie, sources*, 43.

12. Clément, *Athanase d'Alexandrie, sources*, 47.

13. Clément, *Athanase d'Alexandrie, sources*, 48.

14. Clément, *Athanase d'Alexandrie, sources*, 48.

the conscious, free personality and of the intelligence; it is the seat of every decisive choice, of the unwritten law (Rom 2:15) and the mysterious activity of God. In the two Testaments, the heart is the place where humanity meets God, a meeting that becomes fully effective in the human heart of the Son of God.[15]

Many associate the human spirit with the realm of thought, with being gifted intellectually, with being witty. This is the reason for adopting a further expression, "the deep heart," to speak of the core of our being. Everything the scriptures and the message of Christ teach about the heart calls us to one fundamental, essential task: *Go into your room, into the most private place* (Matt 6:6). We might translate this, "Go into the secret place known to you alone, where you can be sure of being yourself and of being known in truth. This is where encounter with God will begin for you."[16] *Coming to himself, he said . . . I will go to my Father* (Luke 15:17, 18). Some spiritual authors talk about the center, the focal point of the soul, others quite simply about the heart. Saint Bruno[17] and Francis of Sales speak of the deep heart; Theresa of Avila locates the secret place as the final, most interior chamber. Xavier Thévenot defines it as "the existential center which enables a person to act as a whole being and be directed wholly towards God and good." André Louf speaks of it as "the ontological nucleus where we are constantly springing forth from the creative hand of God and flowing back towards him."[18]

The deep heart is not the emotions, the sensibility or the feelings. Neither is it the psyche, the intellect or the reason. It is to be found at a different level. The deep heart may be unknown to us, asleep, shut tight, but it cannot die. Recovering the way is a simple internal act, of recognition, of new awareness. Seek, dig your field, and you will find the hidden treasure.

If we have recovered the way of our heart, and it is truly the dwelling place of Christ, if we live from this center, it will be possible to approach our inner turmoil, the dark corners of our past, without fear. We will be able to get to the bottom of our emotions without being devoured by them, to introduce Christ's presence into the tiniest act of our everyday lives. This is why we are to take the time to make this recovery. It is in the heart that we will experience adoration and prayer. The deep heart is given us so that

15. See *Vocabulaire de théologie biblique*, 176.

16. Laplace, *La Prière*, 33.

17. Founder of the Carthusian order, eleventh century.

18. Louf, *Seigneur, apprends-nous à prier*, 28.

we may enter into communication with God, understand the things of the kingdom, and draw life from its source. Therefore, the heart must be nourished and strengthened by God. It learns to recognize the movements of the Spirit within and distinguish them from those that have their source in our psyche or body; we can decipher the signs, the suggestions that come from within, be inspired by the Spirit, and collaborate with him. The deep heart is engendered, sustained, and nourished by the love of God, God who waters and restores it; it will be grounded and rooted in the living love of Christ (Eph 3:17). If we know how to live from a heart renewed by love, the least of our relationships will be imbued with a very special quality and be transformed, "trans-dynamized." This is the place we can be secure, deeply assured.

The function of the deep heart

The heart cannot fulfill its role unless it is open and given to God, living by the very life of Christ. Then, through prayer, it will "light up from within"[19] the psyche and all our faculties, which can then rely on the source they draw from. They can "lean on a heart . . . which has recovered its depth";[20] they can then become fruitful, being strengthened and directed by the very life of God. There is a flow, a flux of life that is let loose and that expands through the whole being. The renewal that the heart experiences is transmitted throughout our organism and then touches our external world.

All too often though, despite being well established in our hearts and having a real prayer life, we don't know how to set our heart in a right relation with the rest of our faculties. The psyche continues in its own vein, and the heart in its. There is a dissociation. When we follow the dictates of our own small, fragile, sick, dependent, changeable egos, acting out of desire to be another person or to have what is theirs, the psyche is not subject to the Spirit; instead it dominates the heart.

In the Bible, Cain is a picture of the person who allows him- or herself to be ruled by the psyche or mind, not listening to God, who all the while is speaking to his heart (Gen 4:16). Cain had a younger brother, Abel, the two of them the first descendants of Adam and Eve. Both of them brought an offering to God. The Lord had regard to Abel and his offering, but he turned away from Cain and his offering (Gen 4:3–5). Cain was full of pain

19. Louf, *Au gré de sa grâce*, 195.
20. Louf, *Au gré de sa grâce*, 196.

and rebellion, and his anger grew, but we read that in his deep heart God challenged him: *Why are you angry, and why has your face fallen? If you do well, won't it be lifted? And if you do badly, sin is crouching at the door. But you, you are to master it* (Gen 4:6–7). However, Cain made no effort to quiet himself and listen, paying no attention to the Spirit's intervention; he followed solely the motions of his own psyche, threw himself on his brother, and killed him. He fell into such darkness when the event might have proven the point of departure for great cleansing and change, a resurrection after an inner death. Cain's story demonstrates how a heart can be darkened; if it is not nourished by God, it will be by the psyche. It is then parasitical; it becomes divided, loses direction, unable to fulfill its true role; the resulting actions are no longer inspired by the Spirit. It no longer has the kingdom as its goal.

Grace

Grace is God's gift. The words used in Hebrew and Greek for grace signify both the source of the gift (God giving himself) and the effects of the gift in us. Grace is active, it works. It is the expression, the manifestation of the presence of God in his people. Grace is totally gratuitous but it does have a singular goal, that we fulfill our condition as sons and daughters of God. Grace is the working method whereby God helps his people become true sons and daughters. This gratuitous nature does not imply passivity or inertia. Because the goal of grace is transformation and renewal, it is necessary to collaborate with it, to respond and participate in its workings.

Grace precedes us. God always has the initiative: "The efforts of the human person are in response to a grace that is already offered."[21] We begin to engage with this way of conversion because we are called and invited to it—and awaited. Grace is present and active each step of the way, every day of our lives. It is given in abundance to everyone. We are no longer alone or left to our own devices. *The LORD himself marched at their fore: a pillar of cloud by day to show them the way, a pillar of fire by night to light the path; thus they were able to go forward both day and night* (Exod 13:21). The pillar of fire never failed. It is a common and serious error to believe there are times when we operate simply in our own strength and ability, and other times at which the grace of God is able to reach us because of the ground

---

21. Xavier Thévenot, in a personal note.

we have prepared. Grace is at work as much in inspiring us to take the first step as in each subsequent step of whatever sort along the way.

Living out of grace will not happen by itself. No, it is a new way of life that demands a definite and deeply anchored decision, and it is God's grace itself which inspires this choice. It is fundamental to learn to ask for grace and then to recognize and receive it when it is given. We need to be vigilant on a daily basis to rid ourselves of the old clothing of doubt, powerlessness, and lack of direction, ceasing to conduct ourselves as though alone in our struggle with difficulties. Instead we establish ourselves in the certainty that we will be helped and strengthened by grace; we can count on it. It will never fail us, even when lost in the sands of the desert or stuck before the Red Sea (Exod 22:5–31).

If we become fixated on some one form in which the grace will be delivered, as did Naaman the leper (2 Kgs 5:1–15), we risk letting it go to waste. If we are expecting to obtain things exactly in accord with our own desires, we can fail to recognize the interior movement into which the Spirit is inviting us.

Grace always responds to the personal, particular need of each of us. Jesus the Christ is the supreme grace; it is through him that grace is given. We are to live out our journey bathed in, accompanied, sustained, and nourished by the grace of God.

PART TWO

Wounds

4

WHAT HAVE WE DONE WITH OUR WOUNDS?

Now that we are a little less fearful of God and have become a little more familiar with ourselves, we will, in the light of the Spirit, ask ourselves the question as to how disorder becomes established. No one is responsible for their own wounds. We start out as victims. But what have we done with what was done to us?

The first step is to name "that which has done us ill,"[1] and especially all the ills that might wrongly be taken for expressions of love. These are sure to have considerable influence over the way we are structured, and they form the way we relate to ourselves, to God, and to others. An excess of misdirected love can be as destructive as the lack of love or love lost. In order to grow into his or her full identity, a child needs a love that is real, warm, tender, and merciful, but also well-directed, keeping the correct distance, one that recognizes them for who they are and what they can become.

We must then take stock of the fact that we have, necessarily, reacted to any wounding, indeed that we responded in some particular way; and we then must certainly ask ourselves if our behavior has been that of a child of God led by the Spirit.

The wounding can have been experienced in three different ways. If healthily, growth results; if buried, it remains active, unbeknownst to us, and disturbs our behavior; and if infected, it leads us in a wrong direction.

---

1. Basset, *Le Pardon originel*, 245–49.

Our purpose here is not to discuss healthy reactions, those that have not resulted in the suffering being circumvented. Such wounding has been undergone in the truth and light of the Spirit.

BURIED WOUNDS

There are those who have no awareness of the intense suffering that has been their lot, or of the rebellion, hatred, or fear that are lodged in them because of the wounds of their childhood. Just because they have been swept under the carpet does not mean that they are not there. They are thoroughly active and will manifest themselves in some roundabout way, the origins of which will not be understood; and they will bring any relationship low. The way of healing consists in recognizing these very substantial emotions, to bring to light the wounds that lie behind them, and to learn to live through them together with Christ in a correct way.

Recognizing them

Recognition does not necessarily mean reliving events emotionally, and surely not taking action against anyone else. It does mean naming accurately, putting into words, the immense grief, the feelings of hatred, rebellion, fear, and jealousy that may be hidden within us. In the Spirit, as always, we must allow the important events of our lives to rise up where before they had been blocked up as too hard to endure. We must never act as though they didn't exist, or minimize them on the pretext that they belong to the past, or that there are others worse off than ourselves. It's not a question of wallowing in pain or rebellion but of living out this descent and subsequent rising in the grace of God.

We often have considerable reluctance about facing up to our emotions; we blame ourselves for suffering and have no idea of how vitally important it is to take on board the pains and griefs of whatever sort that assail us, and then see them through to the end in Christ. It is normal to experience depression after a traumatizing and painful event; in fact it is necessary for our reconstruction.

This kind of process can take months or years. It is essential that we accept the slow pace of things as we perhaps pass through rebelliousness alone in the solitude of God's presence. We need to watch against throwing ourselves into spiritual things, forcing ourselves in a way which suppresses the expression of pain. Instead, we are to remain patient with ourselves and allow ourselves to be bathed in the mercy that little by little restores us.

Pain that is ignored is likely to manifest in latent states of depression, deep sadness, resentment, or rebellion. Like any buried and unacknowledged feeling, it can affect the body and manifest itself in psychosomatic illnesses.

A similar sense of being blameworthy can also prevent us coming to grips with the violence within us. We have to understand that violence is aggression that "goes beyond measure" and is "unregulated."[2] However, aggression itself is an energy fundamental to the human person and is indispensable to life. It is not something we should extinguish, just redirect.

The first step, then, is not to suppress but to allow ourselves to recognize that we are indeed violent, to admit that we may harbor buried anger, suppressed rage. We are then able to present to the light of the Spirit the roots of this violence and the very subtle forms it can take—covetousness, emotionality, possessiveness, blackmail . . . . Violence against others that goes unrecognized is liable to be turned back on ourselves and then destroy us in one way or another.

In fact, we are afraid—afraid of uncovering pain, afraid of seeing the violence within, afraid of awakening feelings that are deeply buried. However, light and love go hand in hand; the light may reveal things that are incubating, but it is gentle and full of mercy. Normally, if we are to give full expression to things we have tried to forget, we need to have someone there who will hear the whole story through to an end, someone who will help us let the light in, into the shadowy areas of our soul and body. We must be able to tell ourselves that the worst is past and gone, that our lone trial is over—and that the solution is at hand. We often curtail or hide this process, thinking that it is enough just to have expressed in a few neutral phrases an entire period from our past, when what is really needful is to dwell on it at length.

It is quite wrong to believe that recognizing the emotions will lead to judging our parents (or others) accusingly. We do not confuse discernment of an action or behavior with condemnation; indeed, we have a responsibility to discern whether or not another person's behavior is of the Spirit and conformable to the fundamental laws of life. It is quite possible to fully respect one's parents and recognize the failings in their behavior, even while naming them as things that have wounded us. The two attitudes are far

2. Brugués, *Dictionnaire de morale catholique*, 454.

from incompatible, but confusion about this often lies at the source of our inability to grieve: "It belongs to the past, it's finished . . . why revisit it? After all I wasn't as unhappy as all that . . . my father . . . my mother . . . they were OK."

At times, if not always very obviously, God is the target of our complaints, but this is something we dare not recognize. However, Jesus himself, who at no point rebelled in any way, gave voice to his complaint as he died (Mark 15:34). There was nothing but truth in his relationship as a son; he traversed the reality of death, abandonment, and aloneness, had felt the weight of others' violence, and had drunk this cup down to the dregs, all so that a seed of life could germinate at the very heart of evil.

Into the depths of our emotions

We must ask Christ to penetrate into our emotions, to establish himself and go to work. The result is a completely new experience. God is there and we can take on and pass through great internal turbulence, and this will not now devour, rob us of hope, or submerge us. *If you walk through the waters, I will be there, through rivers and they will not go over you; and if you pass through the midst of the fire, you will not be burned* (Isa 43:2). *Fear not, for I am with you* (Isa 43:5). At such a time we are somewhat in the condition of Jesus during the days between his death and resurrection, the period when he went down into hell. He will be mysteriously at work at the heart of our troubles. We need to be there with him.

There is a world of difference between blocking up, anaesthetizing, and burying our emotions, or trying to get through them alone—and getting to the heart of them in the presence of God. To fully experience emotion and to do so in the presence of God is the condition for a redirection of the forces of death back towards life. This is a stage that we really need to go through; there are no short cuts.

The pain may remain but it will no longer destroy us; rather, we will experience it peacefully. The violence will be transformed into creative energy, aggression will take its rightful place, and fear will little by little dissolve into trust.

INFECTED WOUNDS

How does a wound become infected?

Often we take paths that are side roads, diversions, in order to suffer less. Wounds then become infected and bear in themselves the seeds of destruction.

Many of us are unaware that, for the most part, we are not talking here about specific and occasional responses, things that there is no need to be overly concerned about in so far as they are simply done with; no, the issue is definite directions we have taken that lead us towards death and have injured our identity and freedom. The wound becomes infected and we take what we are calling false paths. An infected wound interferes with whole areas of who we are, a little like an abscess that has not been lanced. Something has gone wrong, but we are simply unable to know what, unable to get at the roots of our difficulty; we can see only the symptoms of our disease.

Entire parts of our being have thus gone *into a distant land* (Luke 5:13), like the younger of the two sons in the parable, like sheep that have gone astray (Jer 50:6; Matt 18:12; Ps 119:176). They are cut off from God, from their source. They are neither nourished by nor subject to the Holy Spirit; they are heading for death. It is the word God speaks that will enlighten us as to the course of recovery. Grace enables us to set out on the way back, to change direction. If we are to leave the way of death we have taken, we will have to name it and say when, how, and why we got started on it.

Many draw back at just this point because they don't know what to do with what has become evident to them, not knowing how to recover the spiritual dimension at the heart of their reality, how to link up their life of faith and prayer, the living life of Christ, with the truth about their psyche they are now glimpsing. Nevertheless, the process is simple: it is just to change direction.

Again, it's the word God speaks that enlightens us as to the direction to take, and teaches us how, instead of avoiding the wounding, we can experience it in a way that produces fruit. Grace enables us to pursue the way back. We must begin by renouncing the way of death we have seen as such, and then take a fresh step along the way of life—the particular step we are able to make today.

Leaving behind the way of death and choosing the way of life are both specific, conscious, vigorous acts, and are often the occasion of real spiritual battles. They take place in the deep heart, at specific times, in prayer, and are landmark occasions that we need to guard. This process will touch the infected place, and thanks to this a seed of life is planted, a seed that will develop as time passes—but it is the first step that is essential; the recovery of direction and meaning will produce fruit.

In this way we become aware of exactly what we need to renounce and, in God's grace, we should then be able to leave such things behind and follow the way of life.

Monique was a person who was forever comforting others, so constantly, in fact, that it wore everyone down! She became aware that there was indeed something excessive about this role as comforter, so she opened her past up before the Spirit in order to see the source of the behavior. This brought back to her a precise memory of when, as a six year old, she had lost her mother. She saw herself in the yard of the primary school, seated in a corner and saying to herself, "I'm not like the others: they all have a mummy, but I don't. No one is as unhappy as me, and no one will ever be able to comfort me." Without her knowing it, she was embarking on a particular course—"No one will ever be able to comfort me."

She remembered having refused the proffered help of neighbors and other mums. In refusing to receive help, she instead consoled, comforted her father, who was unable to get over the pain and depression he experienced after the death of his spouse, and this became a role she continued in for many years. In her childhood and then in adolescence, she was both recognized and loved for this role as comforter, and it became the way she would live throughout her life. It was her way of living: "I will never express any sense of need; I might be worn out and run down, but this is of no importance, so long as I comfort others." Nevertheless, a still deeper distortion lay hidden behind this first way of proceeding: "No one can comfort me; God himself cannot comfort me; I have to give comfort in his place." In this way, without realizing it, she took a place which was not hers but God's.

Her healing lay in returning in thought to the moment she had made her choice, and seeking in the Spirit, in the light of what she now knew about God, an alternative way to respond to what happened. At the heart of this intense pain, of the collapse she had experienced, she heard the word: *It is I who comfort you* (Isa 51:12); *The LORD God will wipe away the tears from every face* (Isa 25:8); *[I am] with the contrite and whoever is lowly of spirit* (Isa 57:15).

She now knew that the love of the Father could little by little bring her to peace, comfort her, and send her help along the way. She accepted comfort, permitting him to wipe away her tears. She renounced consoling others in God's place, as though she alone could fulfill that role. She fed on the word she had received, and on a daily basis allowed the previously unknown aspect of God's love at the heart of pain to live in her. Little by little her compassion for others was redirected.

Philippe had at many times in his life pursued inner healing, but he always went through the same process: he would go forward for a while and then suddenly find himself bogged down in powerlessness—"I'm never going to make it, so there's no point even trying." He explained that this was habitual. As we read over his history, he told us that he had been raised by a grandmother whose affection had been reserved exclusively for his little sister. He himself felt deprived of any tender touch. One specific incident came to mind. His little sister was on the knees of the grandmother who was giving her a hug. He said, "Me, me now!" and the reply he heard was, "No, no, not you!" This memory summed up Philippe's experience on the emotional level; we asked him if he remembered how he had reacted. His response was immediate and very precise: "I told myself, 'My little sister is very pretty and naturally attracts love. I am stupid, ugly, and naughty. I never do anything good. There's no point my even trying; I'm lost before I even start.'"

Philippe had set out on a wrong path and thenceforth lived on the basis of this wrong idea, contrary to the word of God, who was now saying to him: *This is my beloved son* (Matt 3:17); . . . *I will say to Lo-Ammi, You are my people* (Hos 2:25). Little by little, Philippe became aware of the pain and rebellion that lay buried within, over which he had spread a veil. He vigorously renounced the choice of death he had made, and found an alternative way out. He could begin to confront an unhappy emotional situation because he had understood that whatever happened he was beloved; little by little he was able to enter his true position as a son of God.

We don't have just one wound. Neither is there one cause at the root of our wounds and difficulties. We mustn't torment ourselves or push ourselves to uncover some foundational event, the consciousness of which would be indispensable to our healing. In the life of the Spirit we must allow memories to emerge quietly, accepting whatever presents itself and set off from there. A memory which comes vividly to mind will gather around it plenty of further information which helps shed light on our experience. *There isn't some one false route* that lies at the source of our problems. We have taken many false routes, and the Spirit will discover these to us along the way, a little like the layers of an onion which are peeled away one at a time.

We have to guard against a simplistic, reductionist view of this process of evangelizing the depths. Just because we have become aware of a bad direction we have taken, renounced it, and taken the first step onward, this does not mean the goal has been reached. Some people get bogged down because they have believed this when in fact they are just at the beginning of a way that demands awareness, faithfulness, and vigilance.

5

FUSION

WHAT IS MEANT BY FUSION?

Each of us is born in a state of fusion with our mother, being undifferentiated from her. This is normal and healthy. It is good for a child to be this
way, firstly while in the womb and then for eighteen months or so. The
mother envelops the child: the child is everything to the mother and the
mother is everything to the child. Fusion like this begins as the natural
order of things, and children that have not known this enveloping motherly
love will be very troubled later because they lack this essential stage in their
lives.

What is abnormal and a source of trouble is fusion that lasts too long
and is too strong. The child then finds itself imprisoned: what was good
becomes bad. The mother and child remain undifferentiated in their re-
ciprocal identities. The child is unable to grow in its own direction, unable
to follow its own desires, and finds him- or herself being dominated by the
mother. In a well-ordered family the function of the father is to confirm
the child in its identity. He it is, in the first place, who is to watch that
the mother and child disentangle and so prevent confusion. In one way or
another he will show the child that incest is not allowed, making the child
understand that "the couple" consists of the father and the mother and not
the child and one of the parents, and that it is not the child's place to make
up for any lack between the parents, but is to forge and follow his or her
own way. He is also to instill in the child the fact that no father or mother

can give being to their child, but that being comes from God; and that, under pain of becoming an orphan, each person has to recognize and make the connection with their "I," their deep identity.

If the father of the family does not fulfill his role and the mother is not aware of the essential law of separation,[1] confusion can be established, and many is the person who reaches adulthood without really having experienced the first vital internal separation, that from their mother. They remain, in a way, in the womb, and they will live out this undifferentiated (fusional) state not only with their mother (or father) but also in most of their relationships. The object of the fusion may change from person to person, but the root of alienation is always there.

In passing, it is worth noting that fusion is more or less necessary in the early days for a couple, but it should not normally last beyond a certain period. If it does last too long, the individual loses appropriate points of reference and their deepest desires are stifled, preventing them from emerging and being integrated with those of the partner. The mixing together is a greater source of anguish than separation.

Together with all this, there is frequently an intense sense of guilt. The least act of liberty can appear as a transgression, a danger to the other, because fusion is often accompanied by an emotional blackmail which is difficult to discern. Out of a false sense of compassion, in order to avoid confrontation, it is quite possible to find oneself completely alienated. The desire for freedom is very strong in all of us, so we risk being pulled apart by a permanent internal conflict, and we may even develop hatred and rebellion towards the person who is robbing us of our freedom, of our most basic desires. This hatred can then be displaced onto others or be turned back on ourselves to our destruction.

While there may be this fusion in love, there may also be a fusion in hatred. If this is happening, one party in some form invades the other. The psyche becomes poisoned by murderous thoughts and internal dialogues, by desires for vengeance . . . and it is chained to the one who is despised. This feeling of hatred is usually carefully and deeply buried. We must dare to bring our hatred into the light of day, recognizing how very present it is and allow it to be indwelt by Christ.

Fusion is something that may be experienced by a child who is born after the death of a brother or sister. In the parents' mind the one may in some way replace the other. The parents commonly idealize the lost child,

1. French *défusion*, literally, de-fusion.

and the living child can begin to wish to be the replacement for the dead child and seek to resemble him or her. This form of fusion will weigh heavily on the child's future.

The parents may fuse with the desire of their own child, and this desire then becomes the primordial factor—and becomes their own desire. The most essential thing then becomes that this be satisfied. The child is all too likely to then either enter the power-grasping omnipotence process, in the illusion that the world will always bend to their wishes, or else experience a sense of disillusion which will be difficult to live with.

Then there are those who experience a reaction against the father or mother whose behavior has been of this type. However, far from being set free by reacting in this way, they are formed in opposition to some other person rather than on the basis of who they are themselves.

The human person needs a model. The child will imitate all it sees in the lives of its parents. It is they who instruct as to what should or shouldn't be done. While this identification is good for a time, the child must then choose for him- or herself, hold on to the good and reject whatever will lead down a false path. The essential thing is to not identify entirely with the parents and so trail along behind them without developing an individual mold.

WHAT DOES THE WORD TELL US?

The word cannot but shed light and teach on the conditions within right relationships. Not for nothing are we given to understand God through the prism of the holy Trinity, the source and model of every relationship. Jesus announced the renewal of every relationship (the kingdom), and he lived this out to the full. It's not enough to be founded, based, on love; the love must be true. *Love one another as I have loved you* (John 15:12), Jesus says, not according to your own habitual ways.

Disordered love leads to so much suffering, confusion, and trouble; it can obstruct the future of another if it is domineering, possessive, and devouring, bringing in its train oppression and then violence and anguish.

The first word of life

Also the man shall leave his father and mother and cleave to his wife and they shall become one flesh (Gen 2:24).

Marie Balmary invites us, on the basis of the word of God, to look deeper into this idea of lasting fusion and to become aware of the absolute necessity of coming out of it. Notably, she proposes a re-reading of the story of Abram, Sarai, and the message of Jesus.[2]

YHWH said to Abram: *Depart* from your land, from your origins, *from the house of your father, for the land which I will show you* (Gen 12:1).[3] The land which "I" will show you, the land of "I–you." Abram was therefore being called to leave the country of his father and his tribe, in an epoch when this would have seemed unthinkable, and instead head for his own interior land, his "I," his identity, to be differentiated from that of his father and mother. He obeyed the voice and undertook this interior way, in pursuing which he would become truly himself, receiving his true name, Abraham, and at the same time become fruitful. *This is my covenant with you; . . . You will no longer be called by your name Abram, but your name shall be Abraham. . . . I will make you extremely fruitful, and will cause you to give birth to nations, and kings will come forth from you* (Gen 17:4–6).

Sarai, his spouse, was called to the same path. *God said to Abraham: You will no longer call your wife Sarai by the name Sarai, but you are to call her Sarah. I will bless her and I myself will give you a child by her* (Gen 17:15–16). This was the promise of God, and so Sarah changed her name, signifying that God had established her in her true identity. She had been her father's princess—the Hebrew suffix "ai" indicating a possessive—but she became Sarah the free, unmixed, and able to leave behind her dependent condition. At ninety years of age, she who had been barren would bear unhoped-for fruit.

Jesus was always very clear as to the way he lived his relationship with his family. At age twelve, the age when a young Hebrew took his place in the religious community in earnest, during a stay in Jerusalem at Passover time, he remained behind in the temple when the group to which his parents belonged had set off back to Nazareth. They searched for him three whole days and finally found him in the temple, questioning and teaching the doctors of the law. He responded to his parents' disquietude, saying, *Why are you looking for me? Don't you realize that I must be in my Father's house?* (Luke 2:49). This day, Jesus established in the clearest possible way, his relationship with his family and with God, his creative source, who he always termed "my Father." He returned with them to Nazareth: his

---

2. Balmary, *Le Sacrifice interdit*, 94–97, 115.

3. Balmary, *Le Sacrifice interdit*, 94–97, 115.

education was not yet completed and he needed to live with his parents. The text says he was obedient to them; he could behave in this way because he had previously perfectly established his position.[4]

There are some of Christ's words that we carefully lay aside because we don't understand their real meaning, so we don't know what they mean for our lives.[5]

> Don't think that I am come to bring peace into the world. It's not peace that I have come to bring but the sword. Indeed I have come to set a man against his father, the daughter against her mother, the daughter-in-law against her mother-in-law, and a person's enemies will be those of their own household. (Matt 10:34–36)

> From this time, there will be five in a house and they will be divided against each other, three against two, and two against three. The father will be against his son and the son against the father, mother against daughter and daughter against mother, mother-in-law against daughter-in-law and daughter-in-law against mother-in-law. (Luke 12:52–53)

To understand the message and life of Christ, we need to know that we are dealing here not with rejection or exclusion but with something quite different, with a way of loving, of being properly ordered, of priorities to rediscover at the very heart of love. The object is to establish the conditions necessary for quality relationships. In fact, the Hebrew translation of the Greek word *machaira* does not in the first place refer to a sword but to the large knife used in sacrifices; this confirms that we are not dealing so much with division as with the separation of elements that ought not to be one flesh.

Whoever loves father and mother more than me (literally, "above" me) *is not worthy of me* (Matt 10:37). We have here a very strong statement which can cause serious offence if interpreted wrongly. Marie Balmary proposes the following, which makes things easy: whoever loves their son or their daughter more than me—which is to say, more than their second birth, with the emergence of their own "I" and their relationship with the "I am"—is not worthy of me.[6] A person who prefers to remain in confusion, non-differentiation, mixture, domination, possessiveness, or false submis-

4. Balmary, *Le Sacrifice interdit*, 106.
5. Balmary, *Le Sacrifice interdit*, 93–100.
6. Balmary, *Le Sacrifice interdit*, 96.

sion, rather than walk towards true freedom with all that this entails of internal change, such a person is not worthy of me and does not bear their cross. Such a person stagnates, immobilized, reduced, whereas Jesus says: *I have come that people might have life and have it in abundance* (John 10:10).

Each human person is created unique and so called to grow in this uniqueness. The first relationship for which we are responsible is the one that we have with ourselves, that we must live out what is different, specific to ourselves. This is the bedrock, the foundation, the first call of life, of God—become yourself! If we stay in the womb, mixed up with mother or father, it will prove impossible to access our "I."

Being unique does not imply being totally independent, individualistic, turned in on self, self-sufficient. We are not to become a little god cut out of the true God, but are to live in and develop into our true condition as a son or daughter of God, through the Son. What matters is to be reborn of water and the Spirit, to find our true source, our goal, our real direction. We must allow ourselves to be loved and fashioned so that in turn we can love in the way God loves us. Every human person is called to this new birth, which is different from our biological birth; it takes place at the spiritual level, it comes from God; it has to be desired and longed for, and is given to those who choose it as their path.

If we remain in a state of fusion, we are idolaters. If we set our father or mother in God's place, it is they who will dictate to us their laws, when we are called to let the Spirit inspire us as we participate freely in his work, collaborating in the appropriate way with him.

In the Bible, this way of interior separation from father and mother is given in the form of an instruction. God's instructions are invitations and always lead to life, but they are given as instructions to underline the importance of what is being said. How many have been able to quit the dependent bond of fusion that held them captive when they became aware that they were transgressing a commandment of God, that what they considered a duty was in reality simply wrong. Obeying the commandment of life from God, and therefore that of an authority higher than that of parents, proved the factor that enabled them to leave behind a misplaced guilt.

The second word of life

Honor your father and mother . . . that your days may be prolonged and you may be happy in the land the LORD *your God is giving you* (Deut 5:16).

For things to be as they should be, then, it is absolutely necessary to separate internally from one's father and mother and not to stay mixed with their identity, but there is also the need to respect them. We are to live with these two essential directives integrated; there is nothing incoherent about the word of God.[7] "It is not said that we should love our parents, but that we respect them. Literally the word used means 'to give them their due weight.'"[8] A child that has been mistreated, that has been abandoned by its parents, will probably never be able to love them affectionately, but must nevertheless recognize them as progenitors; this is a place of respect that he or she is never to take away from them, under pain of severe internal disorder and the destruction of a part of self.

Respect for one's father and mother means firstly not denying the fact of their parenthood, recognizing it, whatever dramas we may have experienced, and not ignoring them as non-existent, at the risk of destroying ourselves. Our parents have given us life, and it is as such that we are bound to honor them. Life does not belong to our parents—it comes from God—but they do transmit it to us, and thus have a foundational role. We come from God and we go to God, but our parents are the passageway. This passage may be rough and have certain consequences, but this is simply not something that can be avoided. Whatever the case, we have to remember both our origin in the flesh and the source of our life.

Respecting one's father and mother does not mean we have to submit to projects or wishes they may have for us; we are not here to make up for their lacks, or to be their all; it is not our place to prevent them suffering; we are not to be enslaved in a form of emotional blackmail; nor are we to remain dependent on them. Respecting our father and mother is to accept them just as they are, with all their past and all their wounds. We cannot oblige them to change, to become what we imagine they should be. We accord them the right to follow their own path and to give us the right to follow ours, and to love us in the manner that suits them. We are to respect the way they choose to live and the path they take in just the same way those values apply to ourselves. We must name their failings without condemning them personally, and not try to hold them to account, an attitude which

7. Space does not allow us to cite in its entirety the study on the Ten Commandments by psychoanalyst Daniel Sibony *Pour une éthique de l'être* in *Les Trois Monothéismes*. The author notes in particular his passage on the fifth commandment (329–34) as "an excellent account of what is a life-giving word." A few extracts and comments follow in the text.

8. Sibony, *Pour une éthique de l'être*, 329.

can keep us in a state of victimhood and serve as our principal excuse. We are not to despise or shun them, we are not to reject or destroy them, nor are we to seek to avenge ourselves on them. If we are able to respect them, it will prove much easier to leave them in the correct way.

HOW TO LEAVE FUSION BEHIND

Then he who had been dead came out, his feet and hands bound with wrappings and his face covered by cloth . . . (John 11:44).

Daring to name clearly the behavior of one or the other of our parents is the first step. The issue is simply not one of condemning or accusing, but of discerning behavior which is not of God. Judgment belongs to the Father. *As for me, I judge no one* (John 8:15), Jesus tells us.

Recognizing the state of fusion for what it is is not enough. Once the false path has been seen, the time has arrived to repent of having entertained an idolatrous condition for so long. Repentance is an extremely active matter. It consists of a complete about turn, leaving behind one path to embark on another, breaking with a wrong behavior. It is a choice, a very firm decision: we stop transgressing and disobeying. The choice is made in the heart and the deep will. It is pointless to worry about the bandages that restrict us or the veil that shrouds our face (John 11:43–44). We simply need to be sure as to the depth of our decision.

It is this that enables us to emerge from the division, the immobility into which we are immersed by the oscillation between "I want to, I don't want to," or "I want to, but I can't." Choice which is made in the deep heart is imbued with strength and grace; it is a source of life and carries in itself potential for energy, for spiritual dynamism, for change. If we are watchful, little by little it will draw our behavior into line; it is the solid rock on which we can lean, a reference point to which we can always return.

We need to renounce a certain complacency, a passivity that lies in living the life of another, satisfying their desires and not our own, and abandon the mistaken security that evades the risks of freedom, of the inevitable confrontations and possible rejection. Abandoning is a precise, conscious act. Perhaps we can remember one or several moments in our lives when we have given in. We need to vigorously renounce the decisions involved and make new choices.

We are to choose the direction life takes. We must create new and right relationships to be lived in freedom, properly differentiated from others and with respect for them. We need to re-establish right relations with those close to us, those who are our own flesh. Yes, we have to separate in order to recover our own identity, our liberty, our own desires. Each of us, in whatever situation we find ourselves, can take a step of freedom, however small. It is possible to live in renewed relationship and it will happen because the grace of God is involved. As we introduce his presence at the heart of any change, into this new bringing to birth, the seed of resurrection is planted. The Spirit comforts us step by step along the way. As we separate internally from one or other of our parents, we must entrust them to God, their true Father. We lay on him their difficult lives, their wounds. Then they are in good hands and secure.

As we really discharge this burden onto someone more competent than ourselves to bear it, we are not seeking in any way to avoid our own path, but rather disencumber our hearts of torment. God watches over them, as he does us.

Jesus said, *Loose him and let him go* (John 11:44). The act of loosing is a simple, strong action by which we choose to separate ourselves from the grip of another and become ourselves. It is necessary to prepare in prayer, setting out before ourselves the word of life which is addressed personally to us. We can pray like this: "Today I free myself from the shadows and the domination that this or that person has had over me, and I now free them to go their own way in the blessing of God, in the hand of the Father. In the same way I free them from any hold that I might have had over them, from the shadows I have cast. And I myself freely follow my own path in the blessing of God, in the hand of the Father." This act leads us out of confusion. The other person is not condemned, only their behavior. We are not leaving them alone in their problems; we bless them and commit them to the ways of God. In no way are we forsaking our parents, but "opening a play of distances,"[9] the condition for real relationship.

The pathway of de-fusion takes place first in the restoration of relationship with our parents, but of course it is pursued in relation to all those with whom in some way we find ourselves to be fused. We then reenact every day the vigorous step we have already taken so that we don't fall back into our own trap, not weakening in the new attitude we have adopted, and eventually our daily behavior will conform fully. Falls are possible and even probable. We don't rid ourselves in an instant of every wound, but each is an opportunity for a deepening of our freedom.

9. Sibony, *Pour une éthique de l'être*, 332.

6

CONFUSIONS

CONFUSION IN FAMILY FUNCTIONS

In a family, each person has their own proper place. No one can engage with impunity in a function that is not rightfully theirs.

Noémie was a young woman who very much wanted to get married. Although she met young men who were suitable, none of the relationships worked out. In the course of an interview we asked her to talk about her relationship with her father. "It was wonderful. We would go camping together, went on outings, to the theater, to the restaurant . . . ." "And your mother, she was there?" "Oh, her! She always stayed at home." Without realizing it, Noémie had bonded as a couple with her father, who, failing to fulfill his role as a father, had not set the relationship on the right footing. He should have made it clear to Noémie and taught her that every little girl loves her father, but the couple consists of the husband and the wife, not the father and daughter. Noémie therefore experienced great confusion and found herself unable to establish a new relationship, and more, there was a sort of taboo formed by her father against a permanent relationship with another man. She became aware that there was a fundamental disorder and that she was transgressing a law of life. She chose to abandon the feelings of attraction she had towards her father, to internally re-integrate her mother, according her her rightful place as spouse, and taking back her own proper place as a daughter, free for another love.

Michel was the oldest son in his family, in which the father was often away from home for lengthy periods for professional reasons. His mother became accustomed to counting on him, and little by little, insensibly, he took the place of his father towards his brothers and sisters, and sought to make up for the lack in his mother's life, taking the place of the absent husband. Later he himself married, and had great difficulties in the marriage. He understood that in some way he had become his mother's husband and so could not be truly present in his marriage. His conversion pathway consisted in recovering his place as a son, and returning to his father his true role. Despite his absences, he was still the father. Michel had to renounce being everything to his mother and wishing to guard her against the pain of her husband's absence. He did become a son again; slowly his liberation took hold.

Anne had a weak mother, unable to make decisions or take any initiative. Without realizing it, as years went by, Anne became a mother to her mother. She took charge of her, exactly like a mother with her child, and she became a mother without having been a daughter or wife. She saw that the role of a mother colored all her relationships, that she existed only by being a mother to others. She had to renounce the role of mother and recover her place as a daughter. She continued to help her mother, but now in a correct way, freely, capable of seeing herself properly.

Agnes came with the apparent impossibility of getting married. Looking over her past, she became aware that her parents' marriage had been a failure from the start, so that her mother's love had been devoted to her. Without her having a clear idea of it, the mother had formed an alternative partnership with her daughter. Agnes had to cease being her mother's companion and recover her freedom, the dimension of life as a daughter; she had to renounce the confused relationship. The moment she understood the ambiguity in her situation, she changed direction, recovered her bearings, and was set profoundly free.

These examples are not what would be termed incest, not in the sense of sexual acts between people who are related; but they are "incestual,"[1] that is, they are disordered relationships and functions within families, that, while not sexual, are seriously disturbing to a child. Psychologists who treat children with problems say that a child is often more seriously affected by disorders of this nature within the family than by a lack of love because they lose their bearings and don't know where they are. How can it be possible to renounce a disordered relationship which still exists if you are unable to recognize it?

1. Fr. *incestuel*; a term coined by P.-C. Racamier, 1989.

It is not possible, without serious damage to one's identity, to completely destroy the image we have of one of our parents.

André, following the divorce of his parents when he was only three, lived with his father, who forbade him to see his mother, who was presented as wicked and unbalanced. Later, his father remarried, and André always called his step-mother "mummy." He never saw his mother again. In the course of an interview, he explained that he experienced great confusion at an emotional level: "Everything is mixed up inside me, as though I had no roots." He realized that he had completely erased in himself any image of his birth mother. Nevertheless, it was she who had transmitted life to him, and, as such, had to have her place, even though later he had been loved in a most attentive way by his step-mother. Neither the same relationship nor the same degree of love subsisted with the two, but he had to bring order to his past, and the awakening involved brought him great peace. He was never able to see his mother, who had died many years since, but the fact that he was able to gain clear internal orientation was enough to set him on the path of restoration.

A child can be loved in a way that is confused about gender.

Joëlle was the last of five daughters. Her father had longed for a boy and was not slow to say so. In order to fulfill this desire, Joëlle proceeded to live as a tomboy and extinguish all her femininity. When she became an adult, she found it impossible to accept herself: "I don't know who I am." The fact of being a woman was an integral part of herself. She had to recover her own internal purpose, and renounce responding to her father's wishes. Little by little she recovered her integrity.

It is fundamental to be assured about and affirmed in our sexual identity. This is not to discount the importance of recognizing and freeing the feminine dimension which is in every man, or the masculine element in every woman; but we cannot enter our true identity except by identifying clearly as a man or a woman.

The loss of reference points can also come from the leveling of generations. For example, parent-friends[2] who wish to experience their children's problems alongside them may well prove the origin of internal disorder in a child who is unable to differentiate him- or herself from the parents.

2. Fr. *parents "copains"*; parents who wish to be friends rather than exercise parental authority.

CONFUSIONS

The Spirit of the living God brings order, light, and appropriate relations, where there is confusion, disorder, and chaos. This is his function; he leads into full truth.

The earth was empty and void, and darkness was over the face of the deep; the breath of God hovered over the surface of the waters, and God said, "Light be!" and light was. . . . God separated the light from the darkness (Gen 1:1–3).

TAKING ON ONESELF THE PATHWAY OF ANOTHER

It may well be that we take on ourselves the responsibility for another out of misdirected compassion; we want to save them from their ills, lighten their burden; we want them to suffer less. This is an undertaking that is bound to fail, and many who follow this sort of direction experience a sense of powerlessness in their lives: "I will never make it." Indeed they will never manage to fulfill the task they have set themselves, and will carry this feeling of weakness around with them through every situation. Each person's pathway is altogether personal and specific, and if we don't follow our own path, no one else can do so in our place.

Always we are bound by this law: each person is unique, so each person has a very particular path to follow. A person who takes on themselves the path of someone else cannot properly follow his or her own. We are not talking about being indifferent—"that's their problem, let them sort it out themselves." However, to take on a burden that does not belong to us, to want at any cost to resolve another person's difficulty, to feel it necessary to find a solution to their problems, to want to keep them from any form of suffering, to make up for their deficiencies, to wish by all means to "save," in our own way and by our own strength—all this looks very much like a drive towards omnipotence camouflaged behind the apparency of giving, of generosity. Our love is to be true, our compassion well-directed. This calls for courage because it is easier to be swallowed up by a false sense of pity than to take the straight path. We are to help, to listen, to welcome the other person, enabling him or her to be who they are, but without taking on their burden ourselves. Entrusting each person to their own way is an act that can be undertaken in truly authentic love.

The prayer of substitution

Many believers practice this form of prayer.[3] They pray for someone's healing or deliverance by proposing to take on themselves the other person's illness or other form of difficulty.

Agnes: "Lord, if you heal my child, I am happy to take the sickness on myself." The child was healed, and Agnes suffered illness after illness, utterly unaware that the choice she had made now imposed itself on her, and that she now obeyed it. Agnes had confused her path with that of her child; she had prayed in a disordered way, without the appropriate distance. Never do we see Jesus in the Gospels requiring anyone to fall ill in order to heal another; it just didn't happen and is simply an aberration. Agnes had to repent of having believed that the illness was more powerful than God, as though God could neither heal nor deliver without transferring the sickness onto someone else.

We need to be extremely vigilant not to lapse into this type of prayer. It is an offence to the God of the living; really it is a pact made with death, with the sickness. We give our unconscious an order which tends towards our destruction and we seriously contravene God's instruction to live (John 10:10). We are never to forget that the first task of the human being is to safeguard the life that has been entrusted to him or her, and not to destroy it. We are not to negate the salvation Jesus Christ brings: he alone heals, he alone took on himself our sins and griefs.

For some, there is a very strong temptation to take on themselves the ills of the world, to allow themselves to be bound up, invaded by the suffering of others, an attitude which can be very dangerous. Once this kind of misjudgment of priorities has been uncovered, it is very easy to disengage from it; it is enough to understand that it does not conform to the message of Christ, and to renounce it. The believer's prayer of intercession is fundamental, but it is essential that it be rightly directed. The Spirit teaches us to pray in the correct way; let us allow ourselves to be guided.[4]

Reparation for others

There are those who without realizing it engage in a pattern of compensation. They take on themselves responsibility for the faults of a parent or

3. Payne, *The Healing Presence*, 218–29.
4. One form of intercessory prayer is described in chapter 14 (p. 158).

another forbear, quite unaware of doing so. Just as the individual has an unconscious mind, so does the family, and this is the place of secrets forever unspoken. It is above all in families like these, with unspoken secrets, that children set themselves to making reparation for the faults of their forbears.[5]

Pierre had a grand-father who was a priest, but this man had had a child (Pierre's mother) with his housekeeper. This was never spoken about in the family. Pierre, however, endured an unbearable conflict between his marital life and the mission he had taken on board. Without knowing it he had taken responsibility for his grand-father's problem of being torn between a life as a priest and his quasi conjugal relationship. He tried in vain to find a way out of the difficulty, but experienced the same severe strife. Deliverance consisted in bringing the secret into the open, simply recognizing the truth, and entrusting his grandfather to the hands of God.

When there is marital conflict, children who take sides and identify entirely with one or other of the parents are no longer where they should be, in their own place.

In the Bible, in the way Jesus lived, there is an infinite respect for the very specific history of each and every person. Jesus admonishes us that each person has their own path and their own form of access to God: *In my Father's house there are many mansions* (John 14:2). Jesus in no way sought to prevent Judas from betraying him (Mark 14:17–21), and acted similarly with Peter (Mark 14:29–31). He didn't insist, even when Peter simply didn't understand. He just warned the two of them of the pit into which they were to fall, and left them free. After Jesus' resurrection, Peter was told of the difficult future that awaited him. *And what of him?* Peter asked, pointing to John, the beloved. *What is that to you? You are to follow me*, was the response (John 21:21–22). Jesus, Judas, Peter, John—each had his own path to follow.

ILL-DIRECTED PROMISES

Because of false concepts they have of God, some people make promises to themselves, to others, or to God, which lead to death rather than life. They no longer obey the Spirit but the promise they have made, and this will prevent them from developing in their true identity.

---

5. Clearly explained in a work by Anne Ancelin-Schützenberger, *Aïe mes aïeux.*

At the age of twelve, Emmanuel heard his mother say to him, "If you leave me, I will die." He, indeed, promised that he would never leave her. In all that ensued he found that he could never freely commit himself or follow his deep calling, even though he did move away. He spoke of finding a blockage of sorts, an impossibility to give freely of himself as though there were some inner unconscious prohibition. He underwent psychotherapy, in the course of which he became aware of the promise he had made, but for all that he could not disengage from it. During a counseling session, he became clearly aware of the deep meaning of the word of God, of this law which meant he must internally separate from his mother. He understood that he was in no way to make a promise of this nature to a human person, that he was an idolator, and that he needed to obey the Spirit, who was impelling him towards freedom. He was able there and then to renounce this promise. He was immediately delivered. The inner block was lifted and he could give himself to God without reserve. How could he give himself when he was already given, when he belonged to someone else? In the future he was able to follow his own course and form a marital relationship.

During the course of his healing, he saw clearly how he could have reacted differently, another way he could have taken out of the situation instead of launching precipitately into a promise out of false compassion. He could have calmly explained to his mother that this was not a good way to go, that he needed to be free, that together they could create a new relationship. To give way to blackmail, to pressure of whatever sort, can only make both parties unhappy.

Philippe expressed his lack of well-being during an interview: "I don't have my feet on the ground, I float along; nothing really interests me, I have no desire, no passion to live." He said that he had tried many times to escape from this state, but without result. As we went over his past, he explained that his parents had divorced when he was four. One memory came to mind: "I was lying in my bed and I heard my mum say to me, 'Promise me that you will never be like your father.' I promised." We asked what kind of man his father was. "He was joyful, full of life, initiative, a fighter." Without really being aware of it, Philippe had grown up bound to this promise, had done everything not to resemble his father, and had adopted a mode of life exactly the opposite of his father's. His healing was very quick: from the moment he became aware that he had obeyed a misdirected human desire and not the Spirit, that he was involved in a promise that did not conform to God's design, he was able very easily to renounce it and recover the right way—to become himself.

Edith: "If my father is healed of alcoholism, I will join a convent." She did indeed become a nun, but the vocation did not stand the test of time. It was she who had in every way created the call. She had taken no account of the life of the Spirit within her, nor of her most authentic desires.

Elisabeth and Catherine were twins. When they were seven they made a pact, mixing a drop of each of their blood, as children do: "We will never leave each other." When they became students they lived together, but Catherine died of an illness shortly afterwards, aged nineteen. Elisabeth then began to experience an attraction for death that she could not explain and the impulse was so strong that she began to fear she would act on it; she no longer had any taste for life. She was in fact bound by the promise she had made as a child: she could not leave her sister and sought to join her in death, no longer feeling she had any right to life. She had wrongly envisaged being a twin, and now had to understand that she was not half of someone else's flesh but was complete in herself, that she was a complete person. Leave . . . go to your own land, in your own name . . . become who you are (Gen 12:1).

At times we make promises, vows to ourselves that bind us just as do promises made to others. Generally, this is the case following some particularly grievous event: "If that's how thing are, I . . . ."

Michèle had been involved in many relationships, but they had all been catastrophic. She suspected that it was she who induced the break-ups, but without understanding what was going on. As we went over her life as an adolescent, she became aware that she had taken a fierce decision: when she was thirteen she had seen her father act with an unbearable degree of violence towards her mother. "If that's how things are, I will never marry." Who would think that such a vow could keep a person in captivity? But how often it is so. Michèle experienced the force of the taboo she had imposed on herself and now had to break.

When we are bound by ill-considered promises, it is not difficult to disengage from them: it is enough to become aware that they do not conform to the will of God, and that it is we who have in every respect created the bonds. It then becomes possible to understand that Christ, who came to set us free, is calling us to renounce them. As we perform this internal act, the bonds are immediately dissolved.

7

DOMINATION

Domination,[1] or a psychological hold, refers to having power over another person in a way that takes away their freedom, imposing on them our own way of life and thought, our directives, our plans, our conception of what they ought to become and the pathway they should follow. Domination differs from fusion. In fusion, two personalities become mixed up in each other and there is no separation: the child or adult remains imprisoned in a womb that prevents them becoming truly themselves. Someone who allows themselves to be overtaken by this kind of fusion no longer has their own desires, but integrates the desires of another as though they were their own. When there is domination, the parties are separate, but there is a seizing of power by one of the parties and the crushing of the other. He or she who undergoes this kind of mastering power becomes dependent on the other, is not free in their choices, and is involuntarily under a will that is not their own. There can be this psychological hold without any fusion taking place, while where there is fusion, there is always domination.

SOME POINTS ABOUT AUTHORITY AND OBEDIENCE

Authority is necessary, as much for a child as for the family as a whole, or any human group; without it there is disorder and confusion. Authority

1. The French here is *L'emprise* and was introduced into psychoanalytical language by Roger Dorey. It has this idea of "domination," of a psychological hold over another person; it has usually been translated "domination" in what follows, rather than, for example, "control."

should be seen as the means, the teaching means, to freedom and as a sign of love of one's neighbor. It is intended to lead to a rightly ordered system, one that results from the laws of life. Well-ordered authority which is beneficent to all cannot be arbitrary, despotic, narrow, or legalistic; it must respect the liberty and responsibility of others, their participation, their fundamental rights. Whoever exercises authority is to serve, not be served. It is so important to be able to discern, to distinguish the correct use of authority from the abuse of power. To persist under the domination of a human person, or to submit to an abuse of power is the sign of a false obedience, an alienation from personal freedom. On the other hand, refusing servitude does not mean obeying no one or being completely independent. Obedience has a deep meaning, a basis which is truly spiritual; it is essential to the human person, and to his or her evolution.

The first question to consider is obviously who we are to obey and how. Fundamentally, it is God we are to obey. Obedience is primarily the place of listening: it is to "sit under" or "submit to," to incline the ear, to listen. *Morning by morning, He awakens my ear so that I might listen as a disciple* (Isa 50:4). This supposes that we are available to God for him to literally open our ears, that we desire this, seek it, and give of our time.

Obedience means holding fast to whatever light we have received, and putting it into practice. It is the deepest form of liberty, and while this can seem strange, understood only with difficulty, it is nevertheless an essential reality. In fact, obedience is a choice and a sign of our liberty; we obey because we choose to obey.[2] Choice always has its origin in desire; true obedience is voluntary; it cannot be passive, forced, or grievous. Through love, God gives his laws to his people, he gives himself, and it is through love that we choose to enter the same mode of life, in obedient relationship with him. It is not simply a matter of observing the laws but is a way of being.

I will put my own Spirit within you, and I will cause you to live according to my laws, to keep and to follow my ways (Ezek 36:27). This promise was to find its full realization at Pentecost. A very particular relationship with Christ was created at that point, not the relationship of a slave, a subordinate, but a friend. *You are my friends if you do as I command* (John 15:14). This has nothing to do with our normal ideas of obedience but belongs to a different dynamic; it is where we are to find our happiness, our fullness, our stability. Christ, what is more, *is* the way, and it is through him that it will prove possible to enter this fundamental obedience. He has walked this

2. Bruguès, *Dictionnaire de morale catholique*, 293.

road, this way of being, of living in joy, a joy no one could take away from him, even in the midst of the most intense sorrows and heartbreak. He occupied the correct position. *The Father is greater than me* (John 14:28). This is the foundation of all obedience.

Since, however, we are currently in the flesh, obedience cannot be thought of only in relation to the Father, the Son, and the Spirit, even though this is our base. No, obedience comes to us "in a cascade of mediations since mediation is part of the divine economy. God wishes to save people through people who themselves need to be saved."[3]

It is at this junction of obedience to God and obedience to human authority that we often have so much trouble, but this is quite normal. This is because, on the one hand, there is the risk of being tempted by a prideful independence which can lead to short circuiting our obedience to the mediating forms—the laws which are necessary in any group, the conditions of church membership . . .—by electing to exclusively "listen to the Spirit"; on the other hand, we can engage in a false obedience out of fear, which leads to our being crushed in an ill-directed submissiveness, in running ourselves down, in a misplaced, childish confidence in others through cowardice or laziness, and finally in a lack of discernment . . . .

Christ invites his followers to experience a particular relationship in his body, the community of believers, and he has provided the conditions for a real fellowship which is neither total independence nor servitude or irresponsibility.

WHAT KINDS OF DOMINATION HAVE WE EXPERIENCED?

Many have known authority that is abusive, tyrannical, and legalistic, authority that is exercised apart from its true meaning and they obey in a way that is infantile, childish, full of rebellion and anger. Often adults still live in the fear of another person's power over them, or feel threatened by servitude, are afraid of conflict, or of retaliation! The slightest act of freedom can appear as disobedience, and it is not unusual to transpose this fear onto the relationship with God.

Domination can take place at the intellectual level, but also frequently occurs spiritually, and then it is very dangerous—it is often difficult to detect the abusive use of power when it is presented in a spiritual sounding form or with biblical argument. Seeking help is a good thing, but we have

3. Brugués, *Dictionnaire de morale catholique*, 293.

to realize that no one can discern things for us. It is often through a form of laxity that some people fall into this sort of spiritual domination:[4] it can be so much easier to rely on the discernment of someone or other to tell us what to do to fulfill the will of God, or to lazily allow them to impose their thoughts and decisions.

In this way whole groups can be subject to a domination that is both fascinating and seductive; this is why it is wise always to allow for some oversight of a group by someone from the outside, a person who can warn against this kind of development, which normally is very insidious.[5] It is imperative to discern correctly and not to become complicit in error, in manipulation, in power trips. This is not so much a question of sects in which one man or woman exercises absolute power over others, but of communities that are healthy in other ways, but in which vigilance can become dormant.

It is also important to discern the abuse of power exercised by people who say of themselves that they are weak, and finally come to impose themselves by this means on a relationship, on a whole family or a community; the power of the feeble is often tyrannical. The whole group eventually bows to their demands, out of fear of squashing them; it is essential to leave behind a false sense of compassion, which can produce serious consequences in a relationship.

Quite equally, there can be an abuse of power in the form of overprotection; this can imprison others.

Then there are those who take the word of some human person as an absolute, a determining, a definition of themselves. They assimilate this as truth, without discernment, when in fact it is false and contrary to the word of God. A poisonous seed is planted, and the toxin will spread. It is far from uncommon for this to become one of the causes of the way we run ourselves down: "As for you, you're a bad boy"; "My poor girl, you're not pretty and will never marry"; "You can never have a baby, you aren't strong enough"; "You're no good at anything"; "A woman needs to be independent, self-reliant—marriage serves only to crush"; "When you've had parents who divorced, you're likely to be divorced yourself"; "You are unbearable; you will be the death of your mother"; "This child is the devil; if it wasn't for him the family would have peace"; "You're just like your mother (or

---

4. "Control" might follow more common usage, but as noted previously the Fr. *emprise* is distinctly stronger than control.

5. Braconnier, *Radiographie d'une secte au-dessus de tout soupçon*.

father)." On the other hand, parents can set their child up on a pedestal and garland them with all kinds of qualities. This kind of child will live in an illusory, false world, and will probably find it very hard, later on, to question themselves and accept their limitations and failings.

If we are not sure about our identity, we are in grave danger of running to others for what we should discover for and in ourselves and in God. Of course, we don't construct our selves alone; the way others see us is important and can be a precious source of information, of awakening, of comfort. But we must watch against enclosing ourselves in a wrong dependence, against asking some person to give us our identity, when it is God alone who establishes it in the unity of our being.

Finally, people often live in the grip of a misaligned super-ego. In everyone there is what is termed in psychology the super-ego, in which we find gathered together and assembled everything we know about authority and law. If we have internalized something we have experienced of abusive, domineering authority, and if the problem of living under the domination of another has not been settled, the super-ego may in turn become abusive, make excessive demands, and become a real "internal policeman."[6] It is as if we were facing a tribunal which watches, judges, and condemns. Often we mistake this interior policeman for the way God looks upon us; obviously this is catastrophic for our spiritual lives.

THE WORD OF GOD

The LORD is my light and salvation, of whom shall I be afraid? The LORD is the fortress of my life, before whom should I tremble? . . . Though an army come up against me, my heart fears nothing (Ps 26:1, 3).

Do not tremble or fear, do not be dismayed, for the LORD your God will be with you wherever you go (Josh 1:9).

Fear not, said Jesus repeatedly (Luke 12:32; Acts 18:9; Rev 1:17; 2:10).

The word is clear: a son, a daughter of God, a servant of the kingdom is fundamentally a person of obedience but enslaved to no one. *No one takes my life from me,* said Jesus, *but I lay it down of myself* (John 10:18). He was

---

6. "*gendarme intérieur*"; Louf, *Au gré de sa grâce*, 129–36.

free with the freedom of the children of God, in a full and fine submission to the moving of the Spirit. The word points without ambiguity to the old way that needs to be left behind, and the choice of life to be made. It thus leads to repentance; we are to experience a life of true transition, transition from servitude to human powers into free choice and joyous obedience to God. On this basis, we will necessarily be led into acts of vital obedience (to events, to laws . . .), but our freedom will never again be lost.

We belong to God and are on our way to recovering him as the principal and source of our life, the final goal of our existence, and to anchor and assure ourselves in him. To be assured in God means that we have our center in him, that this is where our hearts find their strength; knowing that each second of our lives "he is" and gives us our being.

Each of us is called to locate ourselves at another level than that of power relationships, that of the Spirit. *Not by power, nor by might, but by the Spirit of the LORD* (Zech 4:6).

At the same time as we recover our roots in God, we choose not to let ourselves be under the domination of another, to the particular form of servitude to which we are subject. As always, this choice and determination take place in the deep heart; we become concerned with "I want," rather than "I can't." In essence, we have to find out where our will stands. It matters little if at this point in time we cannot fully act out, because, as always, the choice, the determination, is enacted in the heart and will lead us out of our paralysis, our conflict, our internal divisions. God's grace is there, and is our sufficiency (2 Cor 12:9).

A further act of freedom that we need to accomplish is to untangle ourselves and disengage from the domination of others, and to free others from ours. In this way each person is accorded the right to walk their own path in liberty. On the basis of such internal acts, we cease being dominated by another person.

He will deliver you from the snare of the huntsman (Ps 90:3). *The net is broken and we have escaped* (Ps 123:7).

8

THE WOUNDS OF LOVE

You are precious in my sight; you are of great price and I love you (Isa 43:4).

Do we really believe this? Is it what we experience?

The human person is made to be loved and to love. Love is the source and goal of all life. A child should as the norm be received and then grow in love, but how many failures and wounds there are! How many children have missed out on or lost love, living with the sense of having been loved poorly, not recognized for who they are, their trust betrayed. Everything to do with love is the source of joy, but also of great suffering and wounding; this can be experienced in a healthy way, but the wounds may also become infected and diseased.

Children who lack love have not received what was legitimately theirs, and for the most part come to believe that they are not worth being loved. This is the case with abandoned children, those who are not supported or seen for what they are; with unwanted children, who are not welcomed, and often have no desire to live; with children who suffer injustice (one child being preferred over the others, or parents who wanted a boy or a girl); with those who were only loved on condition they fulfilled some function (as the responsible older child, as the ideal little girl . . .); with those who are victims of an attempted or planned abortion, who may then experience strong death wishes and suicidal attitudes; with those who are subjected to sexual abuse, who have been treated as objects and frequently live with shame, humiliation, and guilt; with children who experienced a love that was suffocating, devouring, and never knew real love. For many of these people, love is something dangerous, from which they need to protect themselves.

When love is lost a child experiences a breakdown. For example, following a bereavement, particularly if no explanation is given to the child, who is faced with intense, agonized questioning to which there is no response; if the child is very young, they can experience the death of a parent as an abandonment. Again, if there is sudden separation that has not been understood; perhaps with the birth of a new baby, the older child is sent to other members of the family, and when he or she returns, their place has been taken by another. . . . Perhaps there is war . . . the parents divorce . . . anything that represents a loss of fundamental security, above all if there is no possibility of talking it all through. It might be a traumatizing stay in hospital . . . the loss of trust through a betrayal, a secret the child has entrusted being divulged. It is possible that the child will close in on him or herself completely: "I will never trust anyone again."

LACK OF LOVE

How do we react when there is a lack of love? For the most part, the answer is "fear."

Children who lack something as essential as love or recognition, security or trust, go through a state of internal distress, which often remains unexpressed, and they become afraid of uncovering this condition anew, of reliving something that is nevertheless past. The intense suffering is always there, but they seek to escape it, to circumvent it by substituting things that do not conform to the laws of life, and which, in general, tend in two directions,[1] either to fill the hole so as not to experience it, or to organize life around the emptiness so that it does not suddenly catch them out, so they can retain control.

How do we make up for the lack?

There are a thousand ways to try to fill the hole. Food is one: we stuff ourselves, gorge ourselves to no longer feel empty, which in its extreme form is bulimia. There can be an obstinate quest for the love of the father or mother

1. Winnicott, "Fear of Breakdown."

that was missing; there is the accumulation of things—clothes, objects, money . . . too much of everything, much more than is necessary, so that weighed down with things we end up a slave to them; then there is reliance on the intellect, diplomas, studies, so that there is no end to thought, but everything is centered around the accumulation of information, of knowledge, leaving no free space for anything else; there can be excessive activity and charity with no time for silence, for looking within, for simple friendship; then a profession is something else that can take up the whole of life, and we view retirement or a pause in the professional life with anguish; art, culture, music, research . . . all excellent things in themselves if they don't become the absolute, the exclusive goal of life that takes over the entire being.

Making demands on others to fill our void is a very frequent behavioral pattern. If we missed out in one form or another on the love of one or both of our parents, we are at risk without realizing it of seeking the father or mother in every relationship, and so the relationship is booby-trapped. The other person is loved not for who they are but for what they can bring. If what was hoped for is not given, then we can enter a process of recrimination and judgment; a crisis is then triggered in the relationship.

It is frequently the case that in endeavoring to form a marital relationship there is this search for the father or mother, and this is normal. What is not good is if this search is exaggerated and entirely unconscious, so that the person becomes a slave to this quest for something on which they have no real grasp, a search they can't get beyond.

Organizing life around the lack

Another way to avoid facing the need is to organize around it, whether out of fear of melting down again unexpectedly (in which case we prefer to manage it beforehand instead of fearing it), or because we are simply unable to live any other way. These are much more subtle and hidden behaviors than trying to fill the gap.

It is possible to organize life in many ways. We can install draconian regimes from which we do not allow ourselves the slightest departure, an extreme case of which is anorexia. We have limited relationships, hobbies, money, even when we have a profession that is remunerative; we give up on learning, and the intellect is so to speak shut down; we go over our lacks and past difficulties again and again—for example, a relationship may have been conflicted but is back on a good basis, yet we continue to act as though the difficulty were still there; we mistreat ourselves, not allowing ourselves any pleasure or authorizing ourselves to be happy; we choose a direction of life in which we are sure to suffer lack, in a community that is poor at every level . . . .

Organizing in this way has nothing to do with a true spirit of poverty. The poor in heart have no fear of lack, do not try to fill the void, but know how to live through it in the Father's provision; there is no need to control or to protect self, and there is an acceptance of necessary loss; the endeavor is to keep things simple.

Instead of staying stuck in continually recurring frustration, we must ask the Spirit to bring light. We have to begin by accepting the fact that there are obstacles of our own making and that we tend to close the door to encounter with the very One who *has come that they may have life and have it in abundance* (John 10:10).

What does the word say?

It is pure illusion to believe that the goal of life is to fill up our lack, and that blessing means living without it. We forget that there will always be in every human person an empty space that is in fact a cry to God.

The word teaches that it is not a question of filling the need but of experiencing it with God, and Jesus shows the way. It was not the externals that brought him fulfillment; he experienced situations of extreme insecurity—the circumstances of his birth, the flight into Egypt to escape death, a lengthy silence of thirty years apart from a brief episode at the age of twelve. From the outset of his public mission he was threatened, spied on by fierce adversaries who sought to eliminate him, to put him to death. He was betrayed by two of his disciples, one of whom, Peter, was among the closest. He knew the death of a slave after a night of solitude and anguish as though taking on himself the tragedy of humanity without God.

It is very significant that the first temptation he faced after forty days of fasting in the wilderness had to do precisely with this issue of lack—Jesus was hungry. *If you are the Son of God*, the tempter said to him, *command these stones to become bread* (Matt 4:3); don't allow any lack of any sort. You're hungry, perform a miracle; be yourself, transform the stones into bread and you will be filled. Jesus replied that man is not to live by bread alone but by every word that proceeds out of the mouth of God. This is how, even in the midst of lack, he maintains his integrity, his wholeness.

Also, we see Jesus living in joy and peace of a very particular quality through these needs. He shows us the secret of his heart, that the Father is his source and strength. He lived in a filial relationship with him, imbued with everything that is good, trustworthy, warm, and secure. He thus teaches us how a child of God can, if secure in God, embrace lack.

False beliefs that are truly deadly may have taken root in us. If we have suffered a lack of love, we all too often think that a living, real relationship with God who loves us personally is unthinkable, unimaginable. It is like a world that is foreign to us, a language we don't understand, words that have nothing to do with us. Then, if God is really love, it is a love for others, not for us; if we have not been loved, it is because we don't deserve to be loved. It is our fault; how can we be of interest to God?

We must never forget that there is grace, and that God will change *the desert into pools of water and the dry ground into a fountain* (Isa 41:18). When we understand that the blockage is within ourselves, a great step has been taken. Once our false beliefs have come to light, it will be possible to bring them into line with the word of God. This is the first truth we must take on board; it is straightforward and fundamental. We must not identify the love of God with the faltering love of people. In no way do the failings we have known in human relationships have anything to do with our relationship with God. God is not in the image of our parents. The root of this primary difficulty is evidently that we have created God in the image of our parents, and that we relive with him the mode of communication we had with them. How are we to believe the love of God when our own father (or mother) was non-existent, absent, unworthy, or oppressive?

Just because we have no idea of what a filial relationship might be does not mean that it cannot exist between God and us. We can count on the Spirit to lead us beyond the words into the reality of the relationship to which we are called. God loves the unloved: *I will love La-Rouhama* (the unloved), *and I will say to Lo-Ammi* (not my people), *"You are my people" and they will say to me, "My God"* (Hos 2:1, 23). Each man, each woman is of great price and weight (Isa 43:4), and has the title of beloved (Hos 2:23; Matt 3:17). Our land is no longer called forsaken and abandoned, but becomes espoused, his delight (Isa 62:4). No one is forgotten. He takes tender care of those whom no one has bent over at their birth (Ezek 16:1–14). He makes the Vale of Achor, the valley of cursing, a doorway of hope (Hos 2:15).

The way back

Recognizing our delusion, our false beliefs, is not enough; it is essential that we vigorously renounce them. Each of us can without delay, in the grace of God, take a first step. The essential thing is to get going, not to remain static in powerlessness; to create an opening, to allow ourselves to be receptive. We need to make place for something new, for the possibility of relationship, however remote it seems, to be available for the welcome of grace.

We must accept decisively the reality of our past; the past is past and it cannot be changed. "No one can arrange things for me to recover the father I lost at three, or change the fact that my mother walked out when I was seven." But this decisive acceptance of the reality of the past, of our lack, of the loss of love, is not as simple as it might seem. To accept not having been loved, to have lost someone we love and who represented to us our basic security is a fundamental spiritual passage, a very deep detachment, and it cannot be undergone rapidly since it leads to essential, deep changes.

We must also leave behind the illusory hope that one day our father or our mother will finally change, will love us and recognize us for who we are. We must stop dwelling on our misfortunes, and quit the destructive victim status into which we may have shut ourselves. We need to bring to light the reasons (revenge and other "benefits") why we remain attached to our suffering and rebellion. These first steps are accomplished in prayer; here is the source of profound peace and true freedom. All the energy that was taken up by rebellion, in denying reality, in demanding that others change, is now freed for walking into life. This is the beginning of our new life.[2]

Chantal was twenty-four; she was anorexic. From the moment she was made to do anything she didn't wish to do, she would begin to refuse nourishment. We looked with her at how this had begun. She said that her parents had sent her out to work when she was sixteen, despite being well able to pay for her studies. Her first anorexic crisis had begun very shortly after this. Why? "Because I wanted to show them that their behavior was unacceptable. That is not how to treat a child if you love them." Chantal became aware of this vengeful motivation. She had never accepted what had happened; the wound had become infected and had poisoned her life.

2. Fr. *Pâque*, literally, Passover.

Chantal at this point renounced any desire for vengeance and decided to take up her studies once more.

Myriam experienced intense crises of tears whenever she looked back at her childhood. She would choke and be unable to speak. . . . She was fifty years old. What lay behind these fits of tears? "I just wish my parents could be aware of all the ill they did me." It seemed that this objective could only be reached if Myriam wept and showed to the whole world, including her parents, how unhappy she was. However, any road to healing was blocked as long as she persisted in this attitude. Myriam would not accept her past and remained chained to what had caused her pain. The first step towards freedom was to renounce wanting to change her parents; they were what they were. She had to renounce the vengeance she was unconsciously pursuing, and take her life in hand.

Christ teaches us to let the dead bury their dead (Matt 8:22). The issue again is one of leaving your father and mother, but in another way. We have to leave behind the obstinate and unconscious quest for the love we have not known. In the love of God that is revealed to us, and strengthened by his grace, we become able to grieve the loss (experience grief in that inner process that goes so deep).

It then becomes important to watch against another potential pitfall, that of expecting God to meet our need and in the way on which we are fixated. We may be expecting God to replace our father or our mother, and seek from him special feelings of warmth and tenderness. . . . But this is not the way love heals our emotional life. No, he strengthens it in terms of its true function, directing it into life. He will teach us to stand tall and alive in the midst of our need. Christ said, *Abide in me as I abide in you* (John 15:4); *I will not leave you orphans; I will come to you* (John 14:18). This is not to say that some won't suffer a certain degree of human solitude, but they will be able to deal with it, take it on board, and allow it to become fruitful.

Along this pathway, there are those who may one fine day be invaded, flooded by the love of the Father. For others the way may be much more lengthy, and undertaken in naked faith, as they undergo a progressive reconstruction. However, as we put our whole trust in the Spirit, who has the means to cause us to encounter and live in love, as we entrust the goal to his wisdom, we will be given each step of the way the bread, the wine, the water that we need, because *God provides* (Gen 22:14). Nevertheless, our desire will never be entirely met, and this constitutes in fact a call of God towards more life and more truth.

THE WOUNDS OF LOVE

LOVE LOST

Recognizing the breakdown and presenting it to Christ

A child who has suffered the abrupt, brutal loss of a source of love, of security, will have suffered a collapse, deep distress, a kind of "primitive agony."[3] However, if they retain the memory of the event, they may not be aware of what they really felt, and it is more or less certain they will carry, buried inside, a terror of breaking down, a dread of the brutal emotional pit they have experienced. There will be, even in adulthood, a lack of understanding that this terror belongs to the past and that today it is done with.

In this state of ignorance, it is normal to either fall back into self-protection before anything that might resemble or hint at emotional collapse or abandonment, or else seek to go through the whole thing again in pursuit of another outcome, one which is satisfying. The first step to take is to open up to Christ this area of our past, to properly realize that there was a breakdown through the cruel loss of love. The memory of the event is really there, but completely buried, and most of the time there is a blank about everything we have felt. The violence, the intensity of the feelings is anaesthetized, sealed in. We must not wear ourselves out trying to relive the terror we have suppressed, but rather allow the traumatic memory to emerge in a way that allows the Spirit to enter it. The veil is torn, the fog dissolves, and little by little our experience is illumined and falls into place.

Going over an event again in the presence of God

It is possible to return to a memory with what we now know of the love of God; he takes charge and strengthens, telling us that we will never be alone if we learn to abide in him as he abides in us (John 14:23). God does not promise us immunity from the effects of events that can destabilize us at any moment, but he does say that he is always at the heart of every distress. *He uttered his voice; the earth shook* (Ps 46:6).

Michel came with a problem that was apparently spiritual; he couldn't manage to achieve silence and concentration in prayer. The moment he began to pray he would have the terrifying sensation of falling into a pit, into the void. He lived only in the realm of thought and could not envisage letting go and taking leave of the mental. Little by little he opened up about

3. Winnicott, "Fear of Breakdown," 38.

his past and came to an important event in his life, a moment of collapse he could identify. He was just two and a half at the time of the German occupation; his parents fled and found themselves in great danger as they travelled because of the bombing. Seized with fear, they entrusted the child to a family who were passing by in a car, so that he was suddenly cut off from his parents, with bombs falling, on the way into the unknown with a strange family; this was a complete breakdown of his universe and security. The terror belonged to the past and he had experienced it in the powerlessness of a very young child, but he knew now that whatever he passed through he was never alone: *He who sent me is with me and has not left me alone* (John 8:29), said Jesus. Michel reported receiving a fresh image during prayer at the close of our time together. Christ took him by the hand and said, "You are not alone, I am always with you, wherever you are." This word became his daily food, and little by little replaced the anguishing void.

Stéphane fell into depression at regular intervals, without being able to distinguish the cause of these frequent falls. "It's as if I suddenly fall into a hole, in free fall," he said. Together, we looked to see if there had been some form of breakdown in his infancy. He said that he had had a twin sister. When they were just eighteen months, the sister had taken ill and died within a few hours. Stéphane had been offloaded very suddenly to his neighbors; it was an event he related without any emotion—it belonged to the past and apparently he had not particularly suffered. We took some time to dwell on what he had felt as he returned home and found himself alone, with an emptiness that was terrifying because unexplained: what had become of his little sister, where was she? His mother had never spoken about it with him; all he ever saw was some toys shut away in a wardrobe. Why were they locked away? He focused all his thoughts on this event and understood that the origin of his collapses lay in this dreadful anguish into which he had fallen at the time of his sister's death—of which he had never spoken to anyone. Little by little he committed into the Father's love the intense pain he had felt, the anguish of unanswered questions. His depressions became less frequent and ceased completely after some months.

9

COVETOUSNESS

Up to this point, we have substantially been concerned with our relationship with our parents. However, experiences with our brothers and sisters are just as fundamental: here we find ourselves faced with issues of jealousy, rivalry, competition for affection, recognition being given to one and not another, favoritism. . . . Our position with regard to our siblings is obviously important. Observation says that a child can find him- or herself in a state of rivalry with one parent or the other in the case of an only child, but also with other children.

It is impossible to live and avoid situations that are disturbing, upsetting, painful. They are normal and inevitable, but the issue is one of going beyond them and learning to live on a sound basis, rightly understanding relationships. The wounds experienced within the sibling relationship are often deep seated, long term and deeply buried, and because of this they often become the source of infections.

The Bible has plenty of stories of antagonistic brothers, one of whom seeks to get hold of what is rightfully another's, or to be like him in order to benefit from what is his. There is Cain, whose offering was not accepted by God while Abel's was, and he then murdered his own brother (Gen 4:3–8). Jacob, the younger, tricked and cheated his father Isaac in order to usurp the blessing reserved for the elder, Esau (Gen 27:1–29). Joseph's brothers saw that their father, Jacob, *preferred him to them all, and so they hated him* . . . (Gen 37:4). They wound up casting him into a pit in the desert.

Covetousness[1] can be found through the length of the scriptures. David coveted[2] the wife of one of his generals, Uriah, and set a trap for him to have him killed (2 Sam 11:12). Jesus' disciples were not exempt from rivalry: *"What were you discussing along the way?" But they kept quiet because they had been arguing about which of them was the greatest* (Mark 9:33–34).

The envy, rivalry, and jealousy of the Pharisees and doctors of the law with regard to Jesus led to his death, the death of the innocent. But Jesus took death in such a way that he killed hatred dead (Eph 2:14–16) and definitively brought love back to the world.

THE UNFORTUNATE CONSEQUENCES

At the root of rivalry and jealousy there is covetousness, envy. The result of covetousness is violence. The final "word of life" in the Decalogue forbids covetousness, and with good reason: it leads to death and destruction, of self and others. *You shall not set your eyes on the wife of your neighbor. You shall not covet your neighbor's house, his fields, his servant or maidservant, his cattle, his donkey, or anything that belongs to your neighbor* (Deut 5:21). "The Hebrew root of the word 'covet' is 'to charm, or entice'; do not be enticed by what belongs to another—bewitched, hypnotized . . . ."[3] Don't be enticed by what another person has or is, that is not yours. You are forbidden to be another. Don't be enticed by another's gifts, by their course in life, by their role. Become yourself, follow your own way.

Behind covetousness we find the fear of loss, of no longer being loved or recognized, of being of no value, of losing one's position, but also the desire to have, to monopolize. We want nothing to escape us; we want to be loved, appreciated, and valued like others. We want their gifts, their intelligence, their way of expressing themselves, the charm that captures attention.

This covetousness leads to violence against the other, based on bitterness about what the other person possesses or what they are, and desire to obtain them. It can also lead to alienation from self being displaced onto others; we seek to build ourselves on an illusion, a misplaced imitation;

1. Fr. *La convoitise.* The author's note refers to a working paper by Marie-Madeleine Laurent and Dominique de Bettignies, the title of which can be translated as "This is my commandment that you love one another as I have loved you—identity and the other."

2. Fr. the same word, *convoite.*

3. Sibony, *Pour une éthique de l'être,* 339.

becoming mixed in the other's identity, we want to be what another person is so we can have what they have; we run ourselves down and begin a process of destructive comparison with others.

Louis: "I was seven when my little sister was born. I was playing in my bedroom; my father came and told me, 'We now have a little princess in the house.' I acted as if I hadn't heard. I have the feeling that I was thereafter very protective towards my sister, but I know that I am now in a very bad place; wherever I am I need to be number one; I can't stand sharing with anyone and I live in permanent conflict with everyone." Louis wished to recover what he had lost, the time when he had the tenderness of his parents to himself. His healing consisted in recovering his place as a son in the heart of the Father and learning to live in relationship with others within the limits imposed by the existence of his little sister. He could not have everything or keep everything. If he truly found his own place, then he would be able to leave others to theirs.

Suzanne: "I am the fourth in a family of seven. My mother was overwhelmed. Materially, we had everything we needed, but I never knew any tenderness. I was just a number among all the others. The sister after me became seriously ill; for almost two months, the whole family gathered around her in prayer. Today, I understand that at that moment I worked out that the only way to get attention and affection was to be sick. I am forty, and I have the sense that ever since then I have felt exhausted and without energy." Suzanne had to go back in her mind to the moment she chose to be sick; she had to confront the pain of not having been the center of her family's affection, of having been "left out." Now she could allow Christ to reestablish her in her proper place, in that relationship in which she was known by name, in which she could encounter God in an entirely personal way. She became able to renounce her belief that only by being sick and fragile could she be loved and appreciated; she chose to live in good health, even if it meant risking not having the compassion and attention of others.

Envy is murderous, towards others and ourselves. Envy will lead to murder in order to seize another's property or to prevent them profiting from what we don't have or are not. There are many ways to kill others on the basis of covetousness: by devaluing them and despising them; by seeking to destroy their creativity, by undermining them with deceitful ideas . . . . Destructive criticism has nothing of true discernment; based as it is on rivalry, it is wrong from the roots up. This form of behavior is unhappily common in relationships within groups and rarely recognized for what it is. It is also possible to destroy the other by negating their existence, by treating them with total indifference, having an excessively high view of ourselves.

Being envious is one way to self-destruct. By not developing along our own lines we can no longer bear fruit; we are building on sand and have no foundations (Matt 7:26). Then, as frustration mounts, we think of ourselves as victims and will soon dry up as we live constantly comparing ourselves with others. As we seek to prove our value to the point of exhaustion, we begin to entertain feelings of vengeance!

The word of God

Once again the law of life that is transgressed has to do with our individual uniqueness. People who live filled with covetousness are not building their own identity, while the word of God calls them to live as unique, different from and in a correct relationship with others, respecting their differences and not trying to take anything away from them. It calls them to recover themselves. This basic law is found throughout the Bible, notably in the episode concerning the tower of Babel (Gen 11:1–9).

It can only be possible to abandon this competitiveness by recovering our rightful place in God, allowing ourselves to be touched by that specific quality of love that gives no place to preference or competition. Love is given entirely to each person and no one is deprived; what one person receives does not create a lack for anyone else. Love is free and does not depend on achievement or merit. It is enough just to welcome it; everyone is loved, heard, called just as they are, fed (Matt 6:26), built up, known by name, with their needs and past. If we allow ourselves to be loved in this way, as unique, then we have no need to take anything from anyone else. We will have found the treasure, the pearl of great price. Each of us will have to live in the way that is peculiarly our own.

"With each person, something new comes into the world that had never existed before, something original and unique."[4] "Shortly before his death, Rabbi Zousya said that 'in the world to come, the question I will be asked is not "why were you not Moses?" No, the question I will be asked is 'why were you not Zousya?'"[5]

4. Buber, *Le Chemin de l'homme*, 19.
5. Buber, *Le Chemin de l'homme*, 19–20.

THE WAY OF CONVERSION

"Being covetous is to suppose that the other person has taken something of your portion of life."[6] The first step is to find the way back to being within our own self. Being is given by God to everyone; no one can take it and no one is deprived of it. Re-establishing relationship with "being" is a personal matter. Certainly, no one can do it for us, and it is not by taking or by coveting what another has that we can recover being within ourselves.[7]

Being rooted in being is the basis of liberty, of exodus from slavery: no longer are we slaves to the opinion of others, to work, to success . . . .[8]

In order to become ourselves, we have to recognize and accept ourselves within our limits and gifts. We must be assured that all our limitations have been accepted, and that we are not going to fall afresh, along the way, for the illusion of omnipotence.

If we are full of envy then we murmur, as did the Hebrews after their departure from Egypt (Num 11:1). God led them out of slavery, freed them and fed them in abundance as they passed through the wilderness, sending them manna morning and evening. Nonetheless, the Hebrews *loathed the bread of misery* (Num 21:5) even though it tasted of cakes baked with oil (Num 11:8). They wept as they remembered the meat, the fish, the cucumbers, melons, lettuce, onions, and garlic they had in Egypt during their slavery. *We see nothing but this manna* (Num 11:5–6), they said, completely overlooking the miracle they were experiencing. To live each day in a state of gratitude, simply, concretely, as a matter of discipline; to give thanks for creation, for the multiple manifestations of God in one's life, for everything that is good in itself, in others and all around; to habitually have this outlook rather than always being set on what we lack; all this is a true turnaround in our heart.

Nevertheless, it is hard initially to be thankful when serious trials come upon us. Total, deep acceptance of trials takes time; this is a place of suffering and deep detachment, but it is certain that life will spring forth as we submit to the process, and the gift of gratitude will little by little become established.

We must therefore take time to discover our own essential quality, what is particularly our own, to welcome and accept it. How often we would

6. Sibony, "Pour une éthique de l'être," 340.

7. Sibony, "Pour une éthique de l'être," 342.

8. Sibony, "Pour une éthique de l'être," 343

love to have the gifts and qualities of someone else, things that enable them to obtain something that seems so important but that we don't have! Our own qualities are then left unused, persuaded as we are that we don't have them or that they are of no value and not worth developing. Thus do we make a mess of creation! We live alongside ourselves and never manage to discover the real meaning of our lives.

In fact, we start the process of self-deprecation, which produces so many ravages. Of course, this is really a false humility; everyone has some essential quality, which is to be received from the hand of God with gratitude, humbly, and at times with courage, instead of refusing it because we would prefer something else. We are to develop it to the point where it bears fruit. It will not be similar to anyone else. True humility, which it is our real task to achieve, is to know and live up to the measure of our gifting, neither going beyond it nor falling short. Then grace will be given in its fullness and we will be operating happily within our limits.

DARE TO BE DIFFERENT

The way of liberty is a way of differentiation, and true love consists in living out our own difference while respecting that of others, neither denying nor aggressing against them, but without denying ourselves. We often confuse difference and division, and communion with uniformity. We are to live our difference in a way that embraces our own particular role, leaving behind old patterns, not copying what others have done. We are to go forward, initiating things . . . . When it comes to tradition, we need to adopt the same behavior—receiving what is good and true, but always making sure we follow the path laid out for us, which in fact means obeying the Spirit.

The issue, then, is living in accordance with our specific position as sons and daughters of God. This is what Jesus did, fulfilling exactly his allotted task. He sends the Spirit not for us to copy him, but to *do greater works* (John 14:12) than his. We do this remembering all that he said, faithfully, which is to say in the creativity that is mindful of him and is coherent with his message.[9]

We will certainly still find in ourselves thoughts of envy and covetousness, but the essential thing is not to give way to them. Our own function will then undoubtedly emerge because, instead of seeking outside ourselves the ways it can come to life, our departure point is from the center of our

9. Xavier Thévenot in an oral teaching.

being as we live out the words of Jesus—*seek first the kingdom and the righteousness of God and all these things will be added to you* (Matt 6:33).

We will not be able to follow these ways of interior liberty, of return, of deep conversion without painful passages to traverse, but these will lead us to more life. This is something we must know and not be surprised at. Just because everything seems to be going worse after we have gone some way down the road and there has been some awakening, there is no reason to think we are not going the right way; quite the reverse. We are not to fear this kind of suffering, nor are we to take steps to avoid it.

The main source of infection to our wounds is precisely that in order to suffer less we have taken a side road. This is an altogether illusory form of self-protection, a dead-end, the opposite of living, existential faith. The stages we experience along the way are necessary and normal, and through grace we can embrace them; they are part of the spiritual warfare of every person who knows that God lives in them, in each one who has set out along the way. We have to maintain a peaceful attitude; we can't set to rights all our problems, our whole past, not at one go and not in one day.

So, we pass through whatever today brings, and we will be reliving the same steps over and over again in one form or another as we come across new situations. However, from the moment we begin to walk in proper collaboration with the Spirit, we leave behind the ways of death, inertia, and self-destruction. We enter the way of life, of movement, of reconstruction—of resurrection.

PART THREE

How Does God Restore Us?

THE WORD OF GOD

At the home of Mary and Martha[1]

LUKE 10:38-42

As they were journeying, he came to a village where a woman named Martha received him into her home. She had a sister named Mary, who sat at the Lord's feet, listening to all he said. Martha was distracted by all her preparations. She came and said, "Lord, don't you care that my sister has left me to do all the work myself? Tell her to come and help me." The Lord answered, "Martha, Martha, you are worried and upset about many things. There is just one thing that is needful. Mary has chosen the better part,[2] and she isn't going to have it taken away."

As he pursued his mission, Jesus stopped with his companions at the home of Mary and Martha, the sisters of Lazarus, who he would later raise from the dead. They lived in the village of Bethany, and their home was a place of rest and friendship for him.

Martha presumably was responsible for running the house; her sister, Mary, who must normally have had some kind of practical role in preparing food, adopted a position that was unexpected in a woman of this period, setting herself down at the feet of Jesus to listen to him and feed on his words and presence.

---

1. In this commentary on the Gospel, the author points out that she was inspired by the following two works: Basset, *La Joie imprenable*, 207–16; Glardon et al., *Le Temps pour vivre*, 114–30.

2. The Greek here says the "good" part.

95

In the course of this encounter, Jesus taught Martha to live on the basis of being, to discover her truest desires, to choose to have access to what is truly important. Jesus had thoroughly integrated his internal life with his active life so as to be intensely present to those around him, so, rather than think in terms of an opposition between contemplation and action, we can see "a way of experiencing time,"[3] the opportunity given to each person to have access to the deep heart, to engage in the full, rich activity that is a bearer of life.

Martha had some rivalry with her sister, Mary, who, she thought, had something she didn't have but wanted, and was something she wasn't but wanted to be. She was aware that Mary had made a bold choice, and thought of her as having a warm, privileged relationship with Jesus, who recognized and appreciated her, while she herself was forgotten, exploited and probably devalued by virtue of her function.

Mary had chosen to stop and to sit down; "she was focused, both mentally and physically"[4]; she was giving herself to an interior Sabbath; she had "come to herself," like the younger brother in the parable of the two sons (Luke 15:17); she was re-established in her deep heart, and was allowing herself to unfold. She was re-discovering her most authentic desire and letting it take hold, ready to face whatever people might say. She was free, integrated; "she had chosen to be chosen."[5]

Martha was flustered, thinly spread across an excess of activities. She was activated by social constraints, by habit, on automatic pilot. She was a slave to the opinion of others and to her reputation as the mistress of the house; like the elder son in the parable she had grown hard, dried up by duty, which is void of desire, by what she thought others expected of her, and by the idealized image she had formed of herself. She had no idea how to live freely, how to welcome the unexpected, how to take time out to listen to her own vital desires; she no longer knew how to let herself be looked upon and loved, and how to welcome the liberating grace and abundance of God's gifts. Just like the elder of the two sons, she had never dared ask a fatted calf for herself so she could enjoy a feast with her friends. She was alienated and divided, living in one place and wanting to be somewhere else, envious of others' lives rather than building on what she was, experiencing the resentment of an unconverted psyche. She was frustrated, but without knowing why, unaware that she was stifling every aspiration to be

3. Glardon et al., *Le Temps pour vivre*, 114.

4. Glardon et al., *Le Temps pour vivre*, 119.

5. Glardon et al., *Le Temps pour vivre*, 129.

and live to the fullest,[6] and distancing herself from the best within her. She existed in a state of "doing."

"These two women are both inside us . . . and every day . . . these two souls within are disputing with each other, facing off, contradicting each other, and at each instant I can choose . . . ."[7] Jesus heard and received Martha's complaint just as she stated it, but he did not intervene with Mary as she, the Martha who wanted to see the good part she lacked taken away from Mary, had asked him.

As always, Jesus response was personal. Twice he used Martha's name with infinite tenderness, as if to give space for her to not identify solely with her function, but to move on towards her "I," her own identity. He drew her attention back to the fact that she too was loved, that she was valued, but he was also pointing out at the same time that the choice to live was hers alone, and that no one else could make the choice for her.[8] He was helping her bring into the light of day her basic need, the true quest, by awakening her to the existence of a good part—"not the biggest piece of the cake for herself alone, but what no one could destroy or take away from her, that is, her aspirations to be a being, a being in her own right."[9]

PUTTING OUT INTO DEEP WATER (LUKE 5:4)

Up to this point we have mainly been concerned with wounds and false paths. We now go on to seeking to allow Christ to strengthen the most vital areas within ourselves as well as our identity as sons and daughters of God. It is absolutely necessary to underline that God restores by means of the life he gives, but also by his presence and his working in and through the sacraments, the fellowship of believers, the liturgy, ...

These too are essential, indispensable factors in healing. I can only trace out a few of these pathways, so I don't mean to minimize other real manifestations of the love and presence of God, which we can experience in our churches, and which we can go deeper into through more specific reading.

6. Basset, *La Joie imprenable*, 210.

7. Glardon et al., *Le Temps pour vivre*, 129.

8. Basset, *La Joie imprenable*, 216.

9. Basset, *La Joie imprenable*, 215.

10

THE WILL OF GOD

HOW ARE WE TO UNDERSTAND IT?

My food is to do the will of the One who sent me and to accomplish his work (John 4:34); *God is love* (1 John 4:8). This is love for his creation, and a very personal love for each individual. Jesus said that his food was to do the will of God; this was his joy, his motive force, the goal of his existence, so this can hardly be a heavy burden or in any way a duty. No, it is a question of a desire, a life force, a loving response from someone who knows him- or herself to be loved. It is an act of life to do the will of God. However, we are so often scared by this talk of God's will. What will happen if we decide to do God's will?

Perhaps God will want us to do something that doesn't fit with who we are, that is completely beyond us so that we are stretched beyond our own limits. Perhaps we will be obliged to submit to some project that is not of our own making and has nothing to do with our deepest desires. Perhaps what we like best will simply be taken away. Perhaps we will fall sick so that we can learn detachment, or perhaps we will have to give everything away and live in poverty. And then, how actually are we to know what God's will is? How disquieting is the thought of never knowing, or of being mistaken! Is our life to have only the one possible direction, one that we have to discover? Many of us find seeking the will of God for our lives a real torment. However, torment is not God's doing.

Jesus Christ said that he came to free us from disquietude and anxiety; he wished to teach us to live in peace even in the midst of complicated and difficult situations. The will of God can only ever be straightforward, clear, and within our reach. Our allotted task is not beyond our means or achieving; there is no need for us to go up to the heavens or cross the seas to discover the will of God, understand it, and then put it into practice (Deut 30:11).

It is essential that we get light on our faith and not continue in theological error. Misunderstanding what the will of God entails can bring in its train real disaster in our lives.

"The word the Vulgate translated as *voluntas* goes back to the Greek words *théléma* and *eudokia*. These words in turn are used for the Hebrew *rasôn*."[1] The love of God rests on the people he has chosen . . . *You will be called my delight* (Isa 62:4). "My delight" translates the Hebrew word the Vulgate renders as *voluntas*, so the will of God therefore means here the joy the Lord experiences in his people.[2] The closest we can get is with the idea of "desire"; God's desire is that we be a delight to him. This immediately brings with it an idea of personal relationship, which touches all our aspirations, our most genuine desires, our life itself.

God has a design, a desire for the world, for humanity. God's plan concerns the whole of creation, and this plan is revealed in the laws of life, the great laws of the kingdom. We can uncover this plan in God's Word, in the history of the Hebrew people, in the ten words of life (the Ten Commandments), in the teaching of the prophets, in the life and words of Jesus. God's plan is that every living thing have life. However, it is clearly taught that life needs to be ordered if it is to be fruitful. God's plan is that the human person live from and by the Spirit in order to fulfill the calling as a son or daughter of God, fully embracing our humanity.

HOW ARE WE TO DO HIS WILL?

Doing the will of God is the personal response of each individual to God's plan. Each person, as unique, is to manifest, incarnate the plan of God, in accordance with their nature and in a specific way. No one has the same task and it is up to each of us to find the way in which we are to express God's will. It is impossible as well as useless to compare roles; each of us is

1. Louf, *Seigneur, apprends-nous à prier*, 43–44.
2. Louf, *Seigneur, apprends-nous à prier*, 44.

to seek and find our own place, and this will in no way resemble that of our neighbor.

Our desires and dreams

We can't go any deeper into this idea of God's will without thinking closely about the nature of desires in general; the will or desire of God will never contradict our desires and most authentic dreams. It couldn't be otherwise because it is God who is the creator of the desires; the moment we touch on the truth of our humanity, we are thinking about the reality of our being as created by God and saved by him.[3] Errors come because many see the will of God and their own as interfacing, in a way at the same level, whereas the will of God lies behind, at the source and at the heart of their truest desires.

Desire is essential to life. There is life in desiring; if we extinguish desire, we extinguish life. It is impossible to kill, deny, or forbid desire and not court a living death. Neither, though, can we desire just anything or in any old way on the pretext that it is our pleasure that matters first; this leads to destruction.

We need to distinguish between need and desire. With need we have to do with requirements (we have to eat, sleep, and be clothed in order to live), with things we need to consume. When we have what is needed, the need is gone. "With people, however, the need is never purely a need—human need bears the mark of the spirit."[4] Desire too is part of the human person. Jesus teaches that *man shall not live by bread alone* (Matt 4:4). We have to pay attention to needs, to bread, but this is not enough. We are also called to discover the meaning of life beyond merely surviving or the accumulation of goods, and this opens the door to desire. As we discover and redirect our desires we go beyond relationship based on consumption, necessary though that is to life, to a relationship of communion in which each person can be distinct and different while respecting the same in others.

For various reasons we have learned to stifle, extinguish, and kill our desires, perhaps because they are dangerous or because they might lead to risk. They can become too much for us ("better to smother them than let them be seen").

Some people renounce their desires out of fear of living; fear of men or of women; fear of aggression or violence; fear of success, of being happy;

3. Xavier Thévenot in an oral teaching.
4. Vasse, *Le Temps du désir*, 20, "*Du besoin au désir*."

or fear of suffering. "The less I invest in the relationship, the less I shall be affected by a break up, a rupture, a lack, a loss of love." Then there is the fear of risk: "The fewer responsibilities I have, the fewer initiatives I take, the less risk there is."

Often we can think that God forbids desire: "A believer has to do the will of God, and so cannot have personal desires . . . ." Some can even come to think that the fact of being genuinely happy must mean that they are not doing God's will. What an aberration this is! We cannot be other than profoundly happy if we live in full accord with our inner "coloration," with what we were made for, with what we love.

Then there are those who live on the basis of desires that are not their own, perhaps those of a parent to begin with, and then, little by little, insidiously, those of others. Here we return to all the wounds that stem from the fusional state, from domination, from observances constrained by some set of social rules . . . .

Some pay no attention to their own desires: "As long as the other person is happy, that is enough." They are then focused on what they believe to be the gift and concern of others. However, they are no longer able to care for themselves, their life force goes out, and often this habitual stance has its source in an infected wound. There is an imbalance in them, a spring that is blocked up.

Children who were not welcomed or wanted, who were victims of some projected or attempted abortion, may refuse to exist, longing to die.

Many are those who take false paths in order to suffer less and not have to traverse life in its fullness.[5] Their desires are then directed towards a form of death. In fact, we all have within us both death wishes and the drive to live; our task is to develop life and not allow ourselves to be engulfed by death instincts.

Some people do express their pain at having no desire, but here, the fact of suffering means that the life force is not dead, given that the desire to desire is still there. In the light of the Spirit it becomes possible, little by little, to name hopes and allow authentic desires to emerge and become clear. If they are vague or non-existent, then God's desire will encounter nothing but a fog and void. If we think of this desire of God as external, coming from outside ourselves, then we experience interior conflict, and little by little we dry up.

---

5. See chapter 4, p. 46 on "buried wounds."

Predestination

Do you want to be healed? It is unthinkable to imagine those to whom Christ spoke answering him with another question: "What about you? What do you want? What I want is of no importance at all." Nevertheless, this is often what we do. Some of us are so concerned to do the will of God that we have no idea what *we* want, no longer knowing how to think about our personal desires or will. God is not going to desire for us; he is not going to choose for us, decide for us, or live our lives for us. In any case, the will of God does not exist as a decision taken apart from us and what we want, without consideration of our frailties, our limitations, our gifts, as something we are to obey blindly. "The will of God is never presented as an order coming from the outside, not even from heaven."[6]

Often we can think that God wishes us to live such and such a life, in some particular community, in some profession, in a particular country, in a way that has been predetermined and is rather precise—and that we have to find out what this is and then submit to it. We then start asking for and awaiting signs, and these we may well interpret in a way that is really catastrophic and beyond all reason; we take no account of who and what we are, and what we desire.

There is indeed a personal call that God makes to each person, of this there is no doubt. *I have chosen you*, said Jesus (John 15:15). But this calling is in a way an open one. It is the individual response that is to be specific, personal, and unique, one that is creative rather than fixed in advance from all eternity. "The response that we give to God is in no sense one that is written down, not in the book of life or even in the heart of God, except only as an aspiration, a hope for something that God has yet to see and to which we ourselves are to give shape and form."[7] "The will of God is not primarily that you choose this or that, but that you yourself choose as a result of faithful thought, free of selfishness and fear, choosing the most fruitful and most joyful way to live, bearing in mind who you are, your past, your experience, the people you have met [. . .], so, what personal response will you make to the appeal you hear in the gospel?"[8]

---

6. Xavier Thévenot in an oral teaching.

7. Rondet, "Dieu a-t-il sur chacun de nous une volonté particulière?" ("Does God have a particular will for each person?").

8. Rondet, "Dieu a-t-il sur chacun de nous une volonté particulière?" 181 and 182.

THE WILL OF GOD

Adjusting our desires in God[9]

Led by the Spirit we can bring out our deepest desires, but we have then to take a next essential step, to ask the Spirit of Christ to help us purify, direct, and order these desires, to ensure that they really conform to the gospel message, to the life of Christ, to *the word that proceeds from the mouth of God* (Matt 4:4). The desires come from deep within, but at this point of the process it is important to allow the Spirit liberty to work, to learn to listen, to be responsive.[10] The two great temptations are either to fall back into a perverse image of God, with all its consequences, or to refer to our own, unpurified desires as the will of God. We have to be very careful in this second area.

Moreover, in the Spirit dynamics, which are all movement and relationship, we mustn't consider our basic aspirations in an isolated way: we have to relate them not only to our personal reality (our limitations, our family situation, the present situation, our gifts), but to the external realities we might refer to as the theological setting, the setting in which we experience God. This would include the word, the scriptures, the liturgy (which restates the laws of our faith and prayer), the ministry and life of the community of believers, the body of suffering humanity, service to our neighbor, and our relationship to the environment, to the cosmos.[11]

Throughout this journey, we need to feed on the bread of life, submitting ourselves to the life and words of Jesus Christ, allowing time for it all to penetrate.

Jesus welcomed the will of the Father joyously. He demonstrates what a human life can be when we choose to really live as sons or daughters of God, integrating our own most genuine desires with God's, developing our inner liberty in listening and being inspired, in being teachable, in collaborating with the life of the Spirit. This is a mode of life that completely renews relationship, giving it a particular quality, that of a servant and friend. A person whose heart is disposed towards the desire of God becomes a

---

9. The question of the relationship between desire and law, desire and what is forbidden, is obviously very important here. The author refers to Thévenot, *Souffrance, Bonheur, éthique*, 76–81, as well as a working paper by Marie-Madeleine Laurent and Dominique De Bettignies that discusses this theme more deeply on the basis of the parable of the prodigal son, "*Je me lèverai donc, et j'irai vers mon père.*" [I will arise and go to my father.]

10. The word here in French, one that occurs frequently in the following passages, is *docilité*, literally, docility.

11. Xavier Thévenot, in conversation.

friend of Christ (John 15:14). Such a person is creative, alive, responsible, all the while maintaining the listening ear of a disciple (Isa 50:4–5).

TRAPS

Fear of being mistaken

Some people are often so afraid of being wrong, of failing to do the will of God, that they become nervous and skittish. They don't dare take any initiative, constantly living with the hope that the will of God will be manifested to them in some stunning way, and so they live permanently with a form of fear, of false submission. However, it is only their will that can give space for the will of God to be at work. They have to find a correct balance between initiative, boldness, creativity, and responsiveness to the Spirit. This is learned and is experimental. Then there are others who are unable to bear the anxiety of uncertainty and are looking for absolute assurance that they are firmly established in the will of God.

At the moment of taking any big decision, it is absolutely necessary to seek help, but always knowing that no one can thoroughly discern on another's behalf, and that each of us has to determine our own path. There is always a risk of being wrong, so it is essential to try always to take decisions under conditions that allow of true Spirit led discernment,[12] notably by seeking help from someone reliable. If we remain open, we can be sure that the wisdom and love of God will set us back on the right track. At times we may think we are afraid of making mistakes, when in fact at bottom we have not really decided to *do whatever he says* (John 2:5), and our lack of well-being often stems from our resistance to the nudges of the Spirit. Often it is enough just to stop this resistance and commit to having a totally obedient heart, and peace will follow.

We should also remember that in ourselves there is nothing that is entirely pure. Our motives are necessarily tainted by our past and our psychological condition. One of the ways of refusing to accept our limitations is to pursue total rectitude, wishing to be sure that what happens is only and totally of God. It is more or less impossible to discern exactly what is God's

---

12. The author points out that there are books and programs specifically related to life in the Spirit that talk about steps to right discernment. These commonly teach discernment between ideas that stem from our bodies, our minds, and the Spirit. This type of program, she says, is really necessary if we are to become articulate and have clear ideas about life in the Spirit, so as not to be hindered by the various possible pitfalls.

part and what is human. This is our condition as men and women, so let us simply have peace at heart.

It is destructive and false to think that the past is gone and without value: it is experience which enables us to take the new step demanded by today. It often takes a long time, but time itself is one of the limitations we have to accept. This awareness is our opportunity to purify the direction our life is taking. For the most part, as we look at it again, we make new choices with more humility and less passion. Life becomes more true, more alive.

Getting our desires to resonate with God's is as much a fact of the big decisions that will determine the future as it is in daily affairs. This is the way of life of servants of the kingdom, those who have entered into a particular, personal relationship with the Father, with Christ, and with the Spirit.

Devaluing the present

Desiring the present, the here and now, is a wonderful way to live in the will of God. It is also a very profound change of viewpoint, a conscious inner act of a precise nature, a change of heart from one level to another, which enables us to move little by little out of division and flight. The day to day takes on its full meaning. In fact, this is a matter of introducing choice and love into every act instead of living on autopilot, out of necessity, out of habit. We choose to be right there, we desire to be doing just what we are doing, we change the disposition of our heart. In this way, we no longer act thinking of something else or wanting to be somewhere else. Right here we see all our little ways of running away: if . . . when . . . otherwise . . . . The present moment can be fruitful or sterile according to the way we approach it. With no change in outward circumstances, but according to the heart's outlook, it can be imprisoning or full. This is not to say that in certain situations there will be no need for change, and perhaps important changes to our lives, but whatever the case, a first step is to choose to live in the present, whatever it may be.

Each instant is the favorable moment. Each day is the day of salvation. The present moment will never return; why then should we wait to live life to the full, to live happily in the joy of which Christ spoke? (John 16:22)· Why wait to experience love other than where we are now? Why put it off till tomorrow? Where else other than in the here and now are we to seek this presence of the living Christ? Often enough nothing needs to be changed in the present; it is simply a matter of a different disposition of the heart.

It is through stepping back and choosing our actions according to the inspiration of the Spirit that we are freed from agitation and hyperactivity. There is no longer any issue of being constrained; our will becomes fully engaged and the daily round can become the occasion of permanent interest. Our actions are whole, our whole being implicated because the will now has desire behind it. "We don't have time," is the habitual excuse. Jesus was never overcome or stressed in the course of his public life, even when there was no time to eat. This is because he was at peace, one with his desires, living the present moment fully in the grace of God, in love (*agape*).

Noémie worked in a nursery school. In the course of an interview, she said with great sadness that her life had no meaning, that outside her profession she had no service to give that could be useful in the kingdom, and that she didn't know how to use her time to serve God. When we asked her about her life, she said that she loved her job very much. She gave herself to it completely, to caring for children from disadvantaged backgrounds. She knew she could help them and open them up to new worlds. She would meet the parents, and she studied an advanced course to become still more competent, and through all of this she said she had no idea how to serve God. She was constantly on the look out, permanently frustrated. We helped her see that she had a completely erroneous concept of the will of God, and she decided to change her outlook, beginning to receive her work as from the hand of God, as a ministry; her profession became her task in the kingdom. She chose to live each day, working together with the Spirit, watching the work of God being accomplished, a grain of love sown in the heart of the children. She is now full of thanksgiving, fulfilled, having completely stopped tormenting herself.

André was involved in a highly creative, very engaged, and busy professional world. His work colleagues were generous but the lifestyle was disordered. He was the only Christian in the group. He was constantly telling himself that he ought to throw it all in and go out onto the highways and byways to announce the gospel: "There at least I would be doing something important." He also thought that if he was in a different profession, one that was less demanding, he would have time to serve God. He fell between two stools: to stay or to leave—but if he left, where would he go? He was unable to decide, and then suddenly he understood that he needed to give himself completely to where he was, without further ado. He was as ready to leave as to stay, but, given that for the time being he belonged to this group, he decided to be inwardly fully available and totally present. His outlook changed completely; the people around him became flesh of his flesh; he became attentive to each of them, and instead of tormenting himself about how to speak to them about Christ, he asked the Spirit to teach him to announce the message in this world where it was more or less impossible to talk about God. New words were given to him and a whole new field of experience opened up. Little by little he understood how he could open tracks, open doorways, lead to the vital issues, listen. He no longer thought about leaving; his task was here and he consecrated himself to it with all his being.

The will of God in specific situations

How are we to act in a situation that does not conform to God's will and that it is impossible to desire? Situations that are caused by sin, whether ours or that of others, by war, by sickness, by strife—these are not the will of God. It is not God's will that such things occur, but his will does find expression in the way we are called upon to deal with them in the Spirit, in the way we are called to humanize the world, to build what can be built.

God's servants, the prophets, as well as Jesus and his parents, experienced times of blessing, but also serious, dangerous, threatening events that came about through the indifference, the cruelty, the intolerance of those around them, and not from God. We often suppose that the will of God was manifest to them in ways which were perfectly clear, sharp, and immediate, but it is highly probable that they groped around, praying at length to understand what the Father was saying to them through the circumstances, allowing themselves to be guided step by step so that what might have been absurd or simply catastrophic could eventuate in good fruit. They teach us how to experience events in God that do not conform to his will. The condemnation and death of Jesus oblige us to face up, without any possible way out, to our conception of God's will. As we leave behind any notion of God as perverse, we will be much freer to contemplate the way in which Jesus experienced an event that, of itself, was not what God wished for.

The scripture tells us that *Jesus was then leaving this world and going to the Father* (John 13:1), which is to say that he was not facing circumstances in the spirit of the world (despair, rebellion, revenge, trading blows, and so taking the same ground as the adversary) but according to the Spirit of the living God, that is, sorrowfully, but at the same time with forgiveness, with an open heart, and in relationship with the Father who accompanied him through this time of solitude and abandonment. He brought love to bear at the heart of the hatred around him. We too are called to "leave this world for the Father," not just at the moment of our death but daily, each time we are confronted by evil (which cannot come from God). If this is how we act, the power of destruction and death that evil brings will be transformed, and a form of resurrection will take place, life springing forth out of death.

In a very simple way, we can say that doing the will of God consists in learning to experience the least of our actions in the light of the Spirit. We must recognize how often in prayer we ask the Spirit to bring us light, and then, even before our prayer is finished, we go back to our normal way of doing things. We don't know how to open up everything we do to the Spirit, when to speak and when to be quiet, how to behave during conflict, in relationships, in decision making, in our projects. But we can consult him, giving him a chance to manifest, giving him space to speak and be understood. This supposes that we are able to be quiet in order to listen and be taught by the wisdom of God.

This life in the Spirit should be experienced naturally, flexibly, without tension. There is nothing here of introspection or being overly concerned with self. The expectation is that we be ready to abandon our own ideas once they have been made clear; not that we ask the Spirit to confirm our thoughts or plans, but to have a blank sheet, void of our preconceptions, however excellent they might seem; that we leave an empty space to allow the Spirit to manifest and inspire steps that might be entirely unexpected.

CONSECRATING THE HEART

Many of us come to peace in the search for God's will by what we might term a consecration of the heart. On this basis there can be in some form the certainty that our basic desire, our deep will is indeed to live out what God wants. Heart consecration to God will outlast outward, changeable forms. It is altogether possible to live like this in the midst of confusion and disorder if we have not yet found the meaning of our lives or the form in which we should serve.

It may be time to leave behind a group or some form of gifting with which we have been involved for years. Such a departure may be imposed by circumstances, by some life change caused by poor choices, by a lack of faithfulness to some initial good step—it matters little because at that moment we can have this heart consecration, which brings peace and anchors us in what is really important. How many ups and downs, trials and doubts can be avoided if this is how we live. If the consecration is made each day we will not fail to find its outworking, almost without effort on our part. There is no need to wait until we feel all is well and we have disengaged from most of our problems; Jesus chose his disciples in the state he found them, not very enlightened, fraudulent in some cases, not at all honest . . . .

Heart consecration is the most completely appropriate step in our relationship with God, one that we are all called upon to make at some point. There may be areas of our lives that we cannot hand over, but this should not stop us. There are those who wait before giving themselves fully to God, waiting to be able to give up their material wealth and leave everything, to be perfect, to have overcome some enormous difficulty, and so indefinitely put off the act of consecration. However, Jesus never overcharged his disciples but always loved them and encouraged them along the way. God accompanies men and women along their twisted pathways, and whatever the error or fault, we can give ourselves to him without reserve.

This act is intimate and personal; it takes place quite simply in the deep heart, in prayer.

Once accomplished, there is a before and an after. Before, there is the restless questioning, when there is the risk of constantly wondering what the will of God is. After, there is peace of heart, we know the essential issues are settled, and the rest will no doubt follow. The goal of our life becomes to incarnate in our own way the plan of God for creation based on who we are and what we can do. It is as if the responsibility for our path has been entrusted to God; by this action of the deep heart, we become servants of the kingdom. Even if we don't yet know in what way to serve, we ask and allow the Spirit to be number one. There is a covenant with God, a pact.

We must commit to no longer live alone, abandoned solely to our competencies as orphans (John 14:18), but always with reference to the word, consulting the Spirit. We have turned our lives over to God, ready for them to yield fruit. There may be those of us who don't have much idea what use their life is, but our feet are on the road, and there is no doubt that the way will become clear. It is a very deep joy to experience this consecration; a joy to wake up each day with the certainty that "I have found the purpose of my life; I am consecrated to God." Whether we are married, celibate, wondering about our future, this act is foundational. Many who have changed direction, often on the heels of difficulties, setbacks, rejection or abandonment, find themselves utterly destabilized and searching for a new life. Often it is enough just to return to this sort of consecration to re-cover peace because the consecration confirms God's primary gift, without there being any need to incarnate it in some particular form.

11

THE ACT OF FAITH, ANSWERED PRAYER

THE SPECIFICITY OF OUR FAITH IN THIS PROCESS

The evangelization of our depths is founded on a living faith based on the word and the presence of God. In this look at faith we will only open a few lines of enquiry that more particularly deal with our subject. We need to ask ourselves in what way our faith is specific to the journey. In essence it translates into this: *Depart and go to a land I will show you* [. . .] *and I will bless you* (Gen 12:1–2): move towards yourself, towards your roots, your I; I am with you.

Go back to the land of your fathers and your family. I will be with you (Gen 31:3) (the word of the Eternal One to Jacob). Go back into your history, embrace your past. I will be with you. You are not alone on this journey, it is I who invite and call you; I will guide you, surround you, restore you. You are to be confident and set out. *This is my Son, my beloved* (Matt 3:17). I am never alone, said Jesus; and you are not orphans. *He who sent me is with me and has not left me alone* (John 8:29); *Do not fear or be afraid, for the LORD your God will be with you wherever you go* (Josh 1:9); *The Son of Man has come to seek and to save the lost*, which in us means that which is confused, most chaotic, most painful, and most rebellious (Luke 19:10).

There comes a moment in our lives when we have to take a decisive step in this quality of faith, in confidence. We must cease to swing between belief and unbelief, and be rooted into certainty instead of drifting in uncertainty.[1] In fact, we are being called to an act of love in response to another act of love, but to understand this we have to stop associating love with feelings or sentiments, and faith with an emotional response.

Faith is the bridge between God and our lives, and Jesus asks us to act in faith: *Only believe* (Luke 8:50); *Be it done unto you as you have believed* (Matt 8:13); *Your faith has saved you* (Matt 9:22; Luke 7:50; 17:19).

In daily life it is so often only possible to be firmly anchored in faith *after* a period of spiritual battling. This is normal. Many find obstacles in themselves that seem insurmountable; most of these result from wounds that were badly handled and these have repercussions on our faith, all of which needs to be looked at up close in inner healing and counseling sessions.

Nevertheless we must not resign ourselves to a vacillating faith that has no life, that is asleep and is not integrated into concrete reality; it is quite apparent that many of God's gifts are lost in this way.

ANSWERS, OBSTACLES, AND TRAPS

How are we to think about answered prayer as we walk the way of evangelizing the depths? Our starting place is the word of Jesus: *Everything that you ask in prayer, believe that you have received it and it will be given you* (Mark 11:24); *If you believe, you will see* (John 11:40); *I, the LORD, speak and I accomplish it* (Ezek 17:24; 36:36).

We have stressed the dangers of seeking immediate, magical healing, and yet we have these scriptures. How are we to put the word into practice? The first obstacle is of course lack of faith. *O, unbelieving generation*, said Jesus to his disciples who had just blown an attempt to heal a child (Matt 17:17). You failed *because of the poverty of your faith* (v. 20), he told them. Nonetheless, everything depends on the request and the form in which its fulfillment is expected. Many people long for an immediate healing from whatever torments them and demand it forcefully and insistently. However, the truth is that so often they are seeking with much less insistence the evangelization, the conversion of their depths, and frequently this is because they are ignorant of the possible ways to healing: *Seek first the kingdom*, said Jesus, *and everything else will be given as well* (Matt 6:33). This is a fundamental law of life. For the most part they are seeking the everything

1. Janton, *Cette violence d'abandon qu'est la prière*, 43.

else which is to be given in addition, completely ignoring the kingdom, hoping with all their heart that God will intervene without it being necessary for themselves to be brought fundamentally into question and be set straight.

So often we don't hear the answer we are given because we are waiting for something else. "Saint Paul did not obtain what he asked for, but he did receive an answer,"[2] and his pathway of conversion was realized not in the deliverance he was seeking but in a way to live with his difficulty as he stayed in the presence of God. If he had held on tight to the exact request he was making, he would have overlooked the response. It is absolutely necessary to be flexible if we are to hear the Spirit. To the degree that we are fixed on some particular form of healing, we risk missing the path the Spirit is proposing; we then believe he has not answered us, when in fact there has been a full supply, just not in the way we expected. Cain, whose offering was not received by God, unlike that of his brother, Abel, was surely not answered in the way he thought he should be; but God did speak to him, challenging him, as though seeking to help him understand that there was something good to be learned from his trial. Cain, however, did not hear: he was elsewhere, lost in his hatred and contempt, in his incomprehension of what was happening. He didn't listen to the voice of his psyche and walked right past the way that leads to conversion (Gen 4:3–12).

Again, at times we get into an inner condition of waiting rather than exercising faith. Why would we wait to really experience faith? Why endlessly put off jumping in?[3] We are waiting for God to show up when really God is waiting for us.

Genevieve: "This morning I was praying. My first words were, 'Lord, I am waiting for you.' Somewhere inside myself I heard, 'But it's I that am waiting for you.'"

It is good to become aware of the basic fact that it is first of all God who comes down to the human person, who then receives him or her and responds. The father of the prodigal (Luke 15:20) was waiting, looking for him, ran out to meet him, threw himself on his neck and hugged him. Without wishing too much of an anthropomorphism, can we imagine God standing on the pathway home, waiting with open arms, looking longingly down the road, running out to meet us . . . ? Why, how, do we get to this place of depriving ourselves of the gift of God? We have to stay open in

2. Janton, *Cette violence d'abandon qu'est la prière*, 53.
3. Or, "the leap of faith."

some form, but many people, without realizing it, are hoping that something will turn up, a feeling, an emotion, a sign, a manifestation, and if what they are hoping for does not eventuate, they stay at the edge of faith, pursuing their illusory dream.

The act of faith takes place in the deep heart, which is given us to there experience and understand the things of God. Faith is built and sustained in the everyday, so it behooves us to be very vigilant not to allow doubt or a feeling of powerlessness to seep back in.

Often, too, we go through the same process of hoping[4] (rather than acting) when it comes to grace. Many are those who forget to ask for grace, or then do ask and start merely hoping. When they think that nothing is happening, they start to ask again and hope and wait in the same way; this can go on for a long time. But grace is always given; it is the children's bread; it meets their needs, it gives them strength, it is never lacking. How often, though, we fail to recognize that it has been given to us; we don't believe it and don't put into action the faith that will enable us to take hold of it; instead we are waiting "for something to turn up," and we let the grace pass by. To the degree that we ask for grace in some situation, whatever it might be, asking in the Spirit, with the power of the Spirit and conforming to the Spirit's directing, grace can never fail. It is Christ's promise: *Ask, and it will be given you; seek and you will find; knock and it will be opened to you* (Luke 11:9). *Yes, everyone who asks receives, everyone who seeks finds, . . . what father is there among you who, if his son asks for a fish will give him a snake instead of the fish?* (v. 10–11). It is somewhat the same as opening the door to the Christ who knocks: we beg him to come in when he is already there and is just waiting for us to allow him to enter.

THE DISINFECTED WOUND

We do experience the fulfillment of our prayer at every stage of the journey, but perhaps we are not really aware of it. The answer is there whenever we are enabled to open up to the Spirit and receive the visitation of Christ. From the moment we recognize our own blindness and ask God to heal us of it, we are answered. *"What do you want me to do for you?" "Lord, that I*

---

4. The French in this passage is always *attendre* or *attente*, literally "waiting." It can be translated as "hoping" in the non technical sense of vague, indefinite hope that has no real faith.

might recover my sight." Jesus said to him, "Receive your sight. Your faith has saved you" (Luke 18:41–42).

When the Spirit enables us to understand the word in its true meaning, and in his strength, we become able to choose, to renounce transgression in favor of life; then too we receive our answer. In all such processes the answer has to do with recovered freedom. We are no longer bound, and our freedom is functional.

When we recover our freedom, this does not mean that it is complete; it does mean that we can now stand up and take a first step, the step that is within our grasp today. It is for each of us to allow ourselves to be led to discover the fresh step we can take right now.

It needs to be said once again that we have to have a deep acceptance of our limitations, leaving behind an all-or-nothing approach. Accepting with a quiet heart handicaps and frailties that will perhaps never disappear is beyond doubt an act of freedom.

The fulfillment of our prayers also underlies in a very real way every wound that has been disinfected; little by little it will affect every aspect of our behavior, bringing life to the life force.

The infection has disappeared when we renounce the ways of death, which are its source, and choose the pathway of life. A good seed is planted in good ground; it will push through at its own rhythm, becoming the trunk of a tree, the branches, the leaves, the fruit, and little by little it will disinfect the whole being. The pathway of restructuring and restoration of the psyche, of the body, takes effect step by step across time. Some of us perhaps will still have scars, pockmarks, bumps, weaknesses, and physical handicaps because we are in the flesh. This does not mean that there is a continuing state of transgression—we mustn't forget that Jesus, Christ himself, resurrected, still has the marks of his wounds, their scars (John 20:27). However, we experience it all with inner freedom, upright, alive, as sons and daughters of God.

12

THE WORD THAT RESTRUCTURES

THE APPROACH AND THE FUNCTIONS OF GOD'S WORD

Every word of God, each passage of scripture, confronts us with a new way of thinking and living, leading us to an alternative viewpoint, looking in other directions than those we have previously chosen. *If you abide in my word [. . .] you will know the truth. And the truth will make you free* (John 8:31–32). If *you* know the truth, not if *I* know it, said Jesus. We are always personally engaged in knowing the truth.

No one can really know the truth while limited to book knowledge, on a purely intellectual plane. This is a process in which the deep heart is totally implicated since it is there that the word is to be received, welcomed and kept. *As the rain and the snow come down from the heavens and do not return without having watered the earth and making it sprout and bring forth, providing seed to the sower and food to those that eat, so is the action of my word from the moment it leaves my mouth—it will not return to me unaccomplished* (Isa 55:10–11). If we love the word, it will abide in us.

The Word reveals to us the great foundational laws of life. It's in knowing these and understanding their deep meaning that each of us can be clear about the wrong pathways we have taken. As we hear the Word, our outlook and understanding change. We abandon our own wisdom and welcome God's. The Word gives an alternative way out, showing us a different direction than the ones we chose to avoid having to suffer.

The Word is also an appeal, a vigorous invitation to stand tall, to leave behind our imprisonment and take the way of life. *Arise, take up your bed and walk* (John 5:8). *Lazarus, come out* (John 11:43), leave your tomb, your place of death. *Do you want to be healed?* (John 5:6). Don't stay by the tomb, *he is not here* (Matt 28:6). *Why do you seek the living among the dead?* (Luke 24:5).

Finally, the Word of God will restructure the mental and emotional tissue that has been damaged. It now becomes possible to receive the re-structuring word, which is not the same as the word that first got us moving. This new word is "a foundational point of truth"[1] which brings into play a life dynamic that leads us out of anything that confines. It is new, restorative nourishment. The Word will have a tremendous impact on us. It becomes alive. It is for "me." It heals where we are sick. It feeds our will and we will genuinely have food to eat that was previously unknown to us. Little by little, this Word will replace the old foundations with new. No longer will we obey the fragile, immature movements of the psyche, but the word of truth instead.

How are we to fight against darkness and lies except by involving light and truth? The best way to eliminate the old is by living the new. The only way to fight darkness and be freed from an untruthful word is to replace it with the word of truth. The word is the seed of life. If we are able to welcome it, it will become solidly rooted, like *a tree so great that the birds of the air will come to nest in its branches* (Matt 13:32). *I have food to eat of which the world knows nothing*, said Jesus (John 4:32).

At this point along the way, we understand better the difference between psychological techniques (which are of great value and at times indispensable) and the ways of evangelization of the depths by which God restores us through his word. The word will reinstate, reconstitute, regener-ate, recreate our mental, emotional, and physically broken places. *The word of God is living, full of energy, and sharper than any two-edged sword. It penetrates to the point of separation between the soul and spirit, the joints and marrow* (Heb 4:12). The word creates: *Light be, and light was* (Gen 1:3); *Let it be to me according to your word* (Luke 1:38). At this moment the word is truly becoming flesh in us.

---

1. Xavier Thévenot in a personal communication.

HOW IS THE WORD GIVEN?

The particular word that will restructure will be given to each person very personally. The Spirit has multiple ways of making himself understood. At times the word is given before we realize its meaning: we understand that it is for us, but we don't really understand it, and perhaps we aren't entirely living by it. Then, when the difficulty is highlighted, we cry out—"Yes! That was really a word for me!"

Muriel said that she was adrift in life, that she felt insignificant and useless. During a prayer meeting she received a word: *This is my well-beloved child* (Matt 3:17). She experienced an immense joy, but after a few months she fell back into her latent depression, a sort of general lethargy. As we talked she reviewed her past. She was the fourth girl in a family where a boy was wanted, and she had been neither welcomed nor then recognized for herself. She was considered a negligible quantity, and made herself as small as she could so as not to cause trouble. "The further I go into my corner, the less trouble I am and the more accepted, so there is a greater chance of being loved." She was then forty years old, and this was unconsciously the way she lived.

She understood that she should not let herself be conditioned for the rest of her life by a regrettable circumstance of her past, that she came from God and was returning to him, that she could be reborn of water and Spirit, and that through the grace of God she could indeed quit the reduced life she was leading. She remembered that first word she had been given: *You are my well-beloved daughter.* At that moment, not knowing the wrong direction she had taken, she hadn't understood how this word could heal her, set her right, and show her a fresh way out. In a sense she had allowed the word to be aborted. *At your birth, on the day you were born, your cord was not cut, you were not washed in water to cleanse you. [. . .] No one took pity on you. [. . .] Passing by I saw you struggling in your blood. I said to you [. . .] Live, and I made you vigorous as the plants of the field . . .* (Ezek 16:4–7). Muriel now knew how to keep the word and allow it to work in her, meditate in it faithfully every day, and allow it to transform her heart.

In her childhood, Juliette had been a victim of sexual abuse. She felt dirty. She heard the words of Jesus: *Nothing from outside a person can make them unclean by getting inside them; it is what comes from within that makes a person unclean* (Mark 7:15). We explained to her how shame and guilt can invade a child who has suffered this type of abuse. Before anything else, she needed to recognize that she had really been aggressed against and that she was not guilty. The bread of life for her was this: *You will no longer be put to shame or feel humiliated because there will be nothing about which to blush; you will forget the shame of your adolescence* [. . .] *because he who made you is the* LORD, *the Almighty* [. . .] *the one who redeems you* (Isa 54:4–5). Juliette had also been meditating for several weeks on the river of life spoken of by Ezekiel. This river flows from its source in the temple (the deep heart) and births into new life whatever it touches; wherever the water penetrates, it cleanses. *There will be life wherever the flood reaches. . . . Along the river, on its two banks, flourish every species of fruit bearing tree; their leaves never drop and their fruit never runs out* (Ezek 47:9, 12). This life-giving text, which she experienced so vividly, notably in the wounded, bruised, suffering parts of her being, had proved a real and powerful source of nourishment, and had slowly led her into wholeness.

Martine had been abandoned by her partner in marriage. Her heart had been extinguished. The abandonment reactivated serious wounds from her childhood, and the first thing was for her to become aware of these. The word of God wrapped her up in love: *Like an abandoned wife whose spirit is overwhelmed, the* LORD *has unceasingly called you in tenderness.* [. . .] *I will put you back together* [. . .] *with a love without end* (Isa 54:6–8). This was really a spiritual action, and Martine had to watch against a fusional response to God: the tenderness of God had not come to replace that of her spouse, but to restore the area that was wounded. This is not the same thing.

Jean had lived through a great emptiness at the time of his birth. Immediately after the delivery his mother had fallen into a serious depression, which lasted more than a year. Because of this, he, Jean, had been completely set aside for the first fifteen days after being born, and consequently suffered from a serious emotional lack. In the course of many sessions he became aware of the way in which he sought to make up for this lack, notably by intense intellectual activity and constant busyness. He never had a moment to himself. As a child he had let his imagination run wild, which was one way of not allowing inner emptiness; but, little by little, he came to realize that within him was a very deep fear of lack. He had begun to organize around the void so as to retain control: he neglected his relational life, cut down on his interests, ate little . . . . The word which enabled him to step out into restoration was in Psalm 23: *The* LORD *is my shepherd, I lack nothing* (v. 1). Every time during the day that he found himself trying to fill the emptiness or cater for it, he immediately took up the word and this was enough for him to recover a true sense of direction: "I no longer have a need to cater for or seek to fill the need; I no longer have fear because I know the Lord is my shepherd, and even if lack does come, God is there, and all that is really important will never fail. This is my security, my deep assurance."

All these words are alive, nourishing, full of meaning. However, the word can also be spoken as a vigorous challenge, an invitation of a pressing nature, coming to us as an instruction and so in reality as a powerful pointer away from destruction. In this case it is awakening to our transgression and obedience to the word of life, which will lead to our restructuring.

Danièle, following a relationship conflict, felt particularly wounded and aggressed against. She thought she had begun the process of forgiving, having gone through the preliminary stages, notably by shedding light on the way a wound from her childhood had been reactivated, but she was unable to stop dwelling, ruminating, on her griefs and their justification. She asked God to free her from this state, but without result, and every day she was a little further invaded by negative thoughts and feelings. Finally, she had enough courage to stop over the precise problem and open it up to the Spirit; instead of letting herself be drowned, she chose to forcefully ask for light. In prayer, she received a picture: "I saw the grace of God flowing in a torrent through the middle of this conflictual relationship, and all at once, a great rock was there blocking the river bed, and the living water began to ebb away into swampy wetlands." She became strongly aware that her behavior was preventing the grace of God from working freely. Then, during a worship service, she came upon this passage from the life of Ezekiel: *You live in the midst of this rebellious rabble. [. . .] Prepare your bags for exile and leave²* *the place where you are for another . . .* (Ezek 12:2–3). She received this as an order: leave this land of rumination.

This word was so strong that she immediately obeyed and chose decisively to quit the negative state of mind—without troubling herself as to whether she would or would not be able to stop the flood of thoughts and feelings. She explained that she was immediately able to hold fast to this command of life because her sin had been shown her so forcefully. She had previously become complacent with regard to the destructive thoughts and found herself unable to stop them; more—they didn't seem particularly troublesome or serious to her. She told herself that she could scarcely think differently. To her great surprise, from the moment her decision was clearly

2. French *émigrer*, emigrate.

made, Danièle was completely free. If at any moment the temptation came back, she was sufficiently strengthened to be able to quickly dismiss it. "I heard the order to leave. I obeyed and strength was given. The matter is finished."

She then became aware that, although she had experienced important elements of healing, she had not really dealt with her past, and that there remained a latent resentment, an underlying deposit of rebellion that she was holding on to. She understood that the time had come to definitively dispose of it all and stop going over ancient history.

SOME NOTES, SOME PITFALLS

Words that will bring about a restructuring should always be given in the first person so that they can be readily appropriated. They should be brief and to the point: short phrases can be very helpfully called to mind during the day at moments we are tempted to relapse into some habitual fault: "I have no need to organize life around my sense of lack; I know that I lack nothing; He is there . . . ."

It is absolutely necessary to leave the old behind in order to be able to welcome the new. This stage must not be omitted.

In her childhood, Benedicte had been completely devalued. Her mother had left the family home in a state of great emotional disarray when she was just three; Benedicte had been raised by her paternal grand-mother. Because she resembled her mother physically, she was morally identified with her and so grew up in an atmosphere of contempt and judgment which gave root in her to the following belief: "I am a contemptible person, unworthy of love." With her conversion, she had a real encounter with the love of the Father and received this word: *You will be called sought after, a city that is not abandoned* (Isa 62:12). Nevertheless, she said that she had the impression of living in two totally different states; that she knew rationally that God truly loved her but couldn't integrate this reality into her life. There was something like a blockage in her. In reality, she had not disengaged from her grand-mother's attitude, which was very much alive in her and held her in its grip, in fact having more power over her than the word of God. Without realizing it, Benedicte was idolatrous. The moment she became aware of this, she found that she was able to "demythify" this power the grand-mother had over her. Once she had managed this, she could really receive the reformative word that would give her a new name and assured her she was regarded with a quite different attitude, leading her into thanksgiving for the wonderful person she is.

We need discernment as we seek for the new, restructuring word. For this reason it is a good thing to have counsel as we go through the process, to check that we are not falling back into old errors.

Alice was religious. She was a member of a family in which there was a highly conflictual and absolutely unspoken domination and oppression. Her grandmother in a sense possessed her daughter, Alice's mother, who completely dominated her husband. Alice was completely lost in this confusion. In her endeavor to find a way out, she chose to let herself be oppressed, self-effacing so as to keep out of the way as much as possible and avoid the conflicts she could not understand. In her spiritual walk she fed on the word of Christ about the grain of wheat that dies. This, in some form, she said, was the word on which her life was based: *If a grain of wheat falls into the ground and does not die, it remains alone; but if it dies, it bears fruit in abundance* (John 12:24). However, instead of making this a word of life that would help her out of rigidity and paralysis, she was destroying herself. She was burying her freedom, her deepest desires, her gifts and talents. She came to see us in a very poor state at every level. She needed to understand the erroneous nature of her interpretation of God's word. Nothing Christ said could lead to self-destruction. She began to glimpse the meaning of Jesus' words: *I am come that they might have life, and have it in abundance* (John 10:10). She set out on the way of restoration, the evangelization of her depths.

We must pay attention not to manipulate the word to our own ends. Allowing the word to be fruitful, and using it for our own impure goals are two different acts.

Marc was persuaded that his way of healing was to be through the creation of a business. He was sure of success and was far from prudent, but did not think this mattered since the Lord said, *No harm shall befall you and no blow shall threaten your tent* (Ps 91:10). "He protects me in everything I do; I am invulnerable. I can allow myself anything. I don't need to think about my own limitations or the economic situation." Marc was experiencing the first temptation of Christ, and it is exactly where he fell. His business failed and he abandoned any form of faith.

Isabelle's husband left to start a new family. She prayed in the certainty that he would return. The will of God is that *man not separate what God has joined* (Matt 19:6); he could only fulfill a prayer that conformed to his will. She began to wait in a way that gnawed away at her, preventing her from living in the now. She wound up feeling completely exhausted and not knowing how to think about her own faith. The true path was to accept the reality of the event and listen to the Spirit, who would then lead her through the long work of grief to be experienced in the presence of God.

Again, we must not isolate the word. It is essential to set the specific word given to us in relation to the rest of the scripture, with which we need to be familiar and be able to navigate freely. If we isolate a word from its context we can all too easily separate love from truth, and truth from love . . . . The word cannot be separated from considering the life of Christ, his acts, the way he lived (he who is the Living Word made flesh, who experienced God speaking to him like no one else ever could), nor from his living presence working in us by his Spirit, and his presence in the externals of life (liturgy, sacraments, life, and work in our church).

Neither are we to use the word as a form of magic, as a foolproof way to arrange our difficulties. It is not a matter of repeating the word mechanically over and over, but of silently meditating in it.[3]

Obviously, the word that will restructure us can change as we progress. When we have checked out the word we have been given with someone who is able to detect any traps into which we might fall, then we keep it in our heart and abide in it until such time as we know that its work is done. Then, surely, another word will quite naturally be given us, in accordance with our needs.

Today if you hear my voice, do not harden your hearts (Ps 95:8).

He sent his word to heal them and pull them out of the pit (Ps 107:20).

---

3. One beautiful way to meditate on the word on the basis of the experience of Mary, the mother of Jesus, may be found in: Thérèse Glardon, Bernard André, Jean-Claude Schwab, in dialogue with Hans Bürki, *Le Temps pour vivre*.

EVANGELIZING THE DEPTHS

PART FOUR

Forgiveness

THE WORD OF GOD

The parable of the recovered son

LUKE 15:11–32

¹¹ Then he said: A man had two sons. ¹² The younger said to his father, "Father, give me the portion that will come to me," and the Father parted what he had between them. ¹³ A few days later, after getting everything together, the younger son set off for a distant land and squandered all his goods on riotous living. ¹⁴ When he had spent everything, there was a great famine in the land, and he began to be in great need. ¹⁵ He went and hired himself out to a citizen of the land, and he sent him into the fields to watch the pigs. ¹⁶ He would have liked to fill his belly with the husks the pigs were eating, but no one gave him anything. ¹⁷ He came to himself and said to himself, "How many of my father's workers have food to spare, while here I am dying of hunger! ¹⁸ I will go to my father and say to him, 'Father, I have sinned against heaven and against you. ¹⁹ I no longer deserve to be called your son. Deal with me as with one of your workers.'" ²⁰ He went to his father. While he was still a long way off, his father saw him and took pity on him; he ran and threw himself on his neck and covered him with kisses. ²¹ The son said to him, "Father, I have sinned against heaven and against you. I no longer deserve to be called your son . . . ." But the father said to his servants, "Quickly, bring the best robe and dress him; put a ring on his finger and sandals on his feet. ²³ Go and get a fat calf, kill it, and we will eat and celebrate, ²⁴ because my son who was dead has returned to life, he was lost and is found." And they began to celebrate. ²⁵ The older son was out in the fields. When he returned and drew near to the house, he heard the music and dancing. ²⁶ He called one of the servants and asked him what

was going on. [27] The servant told him, "It is your brother, who has come home, and your father has called for a fatted calf because he has seen him return in good health." [28] Then he became angry and wouldn't go in. His father came out, entreating him, [29] but he replied to his father, "All these years I have served you and never disobeyed your orders, but you have never given me so much as a young goat to celebrate with my friends. [30] But now, this your son has arrived, he who has devoured your goods on girls, and you have killed the fatted calf for him!" [31] Then the father said to him, "My child, you, you are always with me, and all this of mine is yours. [32] But we have to celebrate and rejoice because your brother who was dead is alive; he was lost and now is found."

DISCOVERING TRUE LOVE

The two sons who are presented to us in this parable take fundamentally different pathways, but they have in common that neither of them truly knows the Father, and as a result have no understanding of their own twisted ways. One is sure about what he wants, to leave and be somewhere else. The other is certain he has taken the correct route, duty.

Both had lost the way to their heart. One had forgotten it, and the other had grown hard. Neither had really met the Father, neither the one who left nor the one who stayed beside him. (We take the Father to mean God the creator, the source of life, not a biological father.) Both had lost their source. They were not watered by love. They had no inner light anymore, like a pair of blind men. Walking in the night, not in daylight, they were sure to stumble, one into disorder, the other into an excess of order (John 11:10).

The failure of the younger and his unexpected return would shake both of them, the one with distress, exhaustion, and humiliation, the other into rebellion and an explosion of long-held-back anger. The whole event was revelatory to both of them and a possible point of departure for a new life, an open door to recovered meaning.

THE YOUNGER BROTHER

Into exile

He left for the external, *for a distant land*. He thought he could resolve his problems by getting far away from his deep heart, far from himself. He let himself be led by a disordered psyche, which completely dominated him. He had lost any true liberty. He had also removed himself far from the source, from God, and chose to live without any reference to the word, to the laws of life, to the Spirit. No longer was he nourished by the true bread of life, and thus would experience famine both outwardly and inwardly.

His story sends us back to the idea of exile . . . . people. It indicates the way we stray far from God, and the way we build our lives, or allow them to be built, without being breathed on, animated by the word of God and by the Spirit. How many areas of our being have been or are still in exile, cut off from our deep heart, from the source of life, and left fallow!

Return from exile

The younger brother could only experience conversion through return from exile, a return to the center. As always in Jesus' teaching, the way of return is stated in just a few words, very concisely and vividly: *Coming to himself, he said to himself* . . . . He took the road in reverse; he went back towards his heart, towards his source. He abandoned his empty talk and agitation and entered an inner silence. Here we find again the call Abram heard, "Go towards yourself."

The first thing he discovers is himself, his own chaos and disorder. Through this painful and presumably lengthy passage, he emerges from his illusions and discovers the truth about himself, and he recovers contact with his deep heart. In the silence he listens, allowing himself to be taught, and there, digging in himself as one would dig a field, he finds the treasure, the source of his existence, the presence of God, of the Father (Luke 6:48). He didn't yet know him fully, but now there was a meeting. He found a just Father, one who would never chase him away. For the first time he was aware of a sure, stable, solid love, love that was also true.

The inward journey of evangelizing the depths is a return from exile. We are coming back to God. We open up to his light the whole of our past and present. There is no part of us which is to remain in exile; however, we cannot experience this return unless we take time to go within and lead back to the fold those parts of ourselves that are like sheep astray, scattered and lost (Jude 11, 19; Jer 50:6; Matt 9:36).

Becoming aware

"I have sinned." It's because the younger brother began to discover who God is, to see the Father for himself, that he could see himself truly. This is true revelation, not at all the same as exhausting introspection. Because he knew that he would be welcomed, even if only as a day worker, he was able to look back into his past. At this moment of enlightenment he could say, *I have sinned.* He said this honestly, unreservedly, and without seeking to justify himself. He was no longer hiding the truth about himself; his outlook had now changed and he could embrace what he was and all he had been through.

And you and me? The moment has come when, as we look over our lives (because we have encountered light and mercy, the love which comes to meet us where we are in every dimension), we can say, "I have sinned," can take account of our indebtedness, our upended hearts, becoming true and simple, confident and able to receive love.

Getting back on track

He went to his father. The younger brother changed direction; he turned round, a volte-face, the *Techouvah*[1] that is central to Jewish tradition, true repentance. He left the way of death, stopped protecting the pigs. Through God's grace he was able to set out, no longer immobilized by misery, victimhood, or sterile guilt; it was the time to choose, to be decisive.

He recovered movement into life, and was about to make something out of the previous catastrophe. He left just as he was, in the state he was, even though he had not reached a full understanding and his first concern was survival. He was prepared to embrace a most inglorious return, because now he was free, lit up by the word he had found deep within.

The Spirit assures us that, in the grace of God, we can change direction, cast off our old clothing, and enter a new life. We can make something of past events; no longer shut in by the past, it is always possible to take a step into life, whatever our current condition.

Nevertheless, the younger brother was only at the very beginning of his way back; he did not yet really know the Father, but he was about to have an overwhelming experience, far beyond anything he could have imagined. *He was still far away,* far from really taking in all that had happened, and

---

1. Steinsaltz, *La Rose aux treize pétales*, 137–50.

far from a true knowledge of the Father, this Father who was watching and waiting for him to come back, and would see him, be filled with compassion, run out to meet him, throw himself on his neck, and hold him tight. This is when, in the arms of the Father, he would have, even in his flesh, the encounter that would make him a son. His heart broke and was ready to be made anew. "He expected a judge, he found a harbor; run aground, deserted, he was finally ready to be loved. His cheek held fast against his father, like a new-born on his mother's tummy, he had come to birth."[2] *My son was dead and has come back to life*, his father said. He experienced unconditional welcome, forgiveness in the light, Paschal peace: he was alive.

He was therefore taking his place as a son, the inner place the Father gave him and which he gives to each of us, which no one can ever take away. He had received the new Spirit spoken of by Ezekiel (Ezek 36:26).

We have already marveled, as we meditated on the text on the healing of the infirm man at Bethesda, at the revelation that even if we are still far, very far away, the love of God is searching for us, waiting, watching for the slightest sign of an opening. We know now that whatever our condition, in his grace, we can always rise up and make our way back towards the Father. Even if the action we take seems insignificant, it is enough to set us on the way of resurrection (John 5:7; 11:41). It is not our place to look after pigs, nor to be hired workers; through Christ we are sons and daughters of God. We are cared for, informed, forgiven, comforted. We have nothing more to do than open our heart to initiate a feast, to receive the insignia of a son, the robes of a distinguished guest, the ring—the family seal, and the sandals, the sign of the free (slaves went bare foot).

THE ELDER SON

The elder of the two sons expressed his rebellion very vividly: *[I have] never disobeyed your orders.* "Me, I'm perfect, upright, a worker, obedient, serious, thrifty, and it's for the other one, the rogue, that you throw a party, something you've never done for me." The elder son's fundamental problem is that he thought himself sinless. He believed himself to be righteous, and as result saw himself at heart as an upholder of the law. Only a powerful event could reveal his hidden failing. How often is this the way we are revealed to ourselves! Our reaction to some concrete event reveals what is really going on inside us. The elder son symbolizes our blindness to our

2. P. Baudiquey on *The Prodigal Son* by Rembrandt.

most profound distortion, our resistance to living in the light, our good opinion of ourselves. He was full of himself, his own dupe. He had never encountered love, probably because he could not let himself be harried, brought into question. Above anything else he sought a superficial and illusory order. He held himself aloof, alone and joyless, outside relationship and outside the feast.

His pain and anger were normal reactions and it was good for him to recognize them and deal with them, but he had also to ask himself what information they were giving him, what the situation meant to him. Why was there this anger against his father and the decisive rejection of his brother? For him, the important thing was to allow himself to be brought into question, that he take time to consider the cause of the serious insecurity he was experiencing, and that he welcome the profound healing his father was proposing. Unlike his younger brother, when faced with difficulty, he stiffened, reinforced his defences.

He was the grain that refuses to die and so stays alone (John 12:24). His apparent perfection hid a fear to live, a false submissiveness, a refusal to accept the differences in others, an inability to receive the Father's gifts. He had no idea that to enter the kingdom it is not enough just not to transgress, but that a new heart-disposition is needed.[3] He was not creative, not a risk taker. We sense that he was not happy; like Martha he was doubtless full of internal murmuring (Luke 10:38–42).

But of all this he was ignorant; he was blind and he believed he saw.

We may see ourselves in the attitude of either the older or the younger, but most of the time both dispositions of the heart are there.

THE FATHER

The Father threw a party for the son who was lost and found, but he loved just as much the son who had stayed alongside him but had let his heart grow hard. He went out to meet him, to plead with him to join the joy of reunion (Luke 15:28). He didn't leave him to his solitude and refusal; neither did he denounce his sin. The Father goes in search of those who have a heart of stone, who protect themselves, who are jealous, and this is a profound comfort to us all. He enables us to know, to rediscover, how to live from the heart of a child of God: *My child, you are always with me, and all that is mine is yours* (v. 31). It is because of this that we can say, "I have

3. Leclerc, *Le Royaume caché*, 104.

sinned." And then—the tiniest step we take to join the feast is welcomed with great joy.

Jesus told this story to the ordinary people around him, *to the tax collectors, to sinners* (v. 1), who rushed to hear someone who believed they were able to understand the things of the kingdom. But the Pharisees and scribes were there too (v. 2). They pressed in on him, watching him closely, laying traps to catch him; and to them too Jesus spoke, to these men whose hearts so resembled the elder son. He announced to them that the tenderness and welcome of the Father were as much for them as for anyone else. He was trying to get them to see that God could melt their hearts.

We don't know what pathway of cleansing the elder would take; what should be learned from this parable is that we may indeed harden our hearts in an appearance of faithfulness, in sterile observance of law.

COMMON POINTS BETWEEN GIVING AND RECEIVING FORGIVENESS

The forgiveness we receive for ourselves and which we give to others is central to our progress. Forgiveness is a spiritual act; it can only come from God. God alone grants pardon. Forgiveness is the high-point of love, and love is of God, indeed love is God. "Forgiveness is not indulgence; it is factually speaking a re-creation."[4] "It recreates what the human being had de-created."[5] It is of the same order as the resurrection, and only God has power to re-create, to resurrect. Forgiveness is a return to life. *My son who was dead is alive again* (Luke 15:24). It is opening, restoration, a welcome to grace. Forgiveness both received and given is the opposite of turning in upon oneself.

Asking or receiving forgiveness alike lead into a process of renunciation, detachment, and mourning that consists in letting go of our nets, loosening our grip, "unmixing" ourselves from others and from what is wrong; to untie, let go, not hold on, not shut the door. Through forgiveness we are freed and free others,

Forgiveness changes the flow of evil forces. A germ of fecundity, of life, is planted at the heart of death. It is the one act that can turn evil into good, which redirects the forces of destruction towards life. All the energy

---

4. Varillon, *Joie de croire, joie de vivre*, 77.
5. Varillon, *Vivre le christianisme*, 114.

we were expending on recrimination, hatred, seeking vengeance, or was turned in on ourselves, now becomes constructive and fruitful.

Forgiveness is God's response to the world's ills; mercy touches us at the heart of our disorder and it is this encounter which will establish us in truth. Forgiveness comes from God, but we are directly implicated and called to participate. It is we who are to allow the forgiveness of God to be incarnated and bear fruit. Jesus brings us back to the source of forgiveness, the Father, but he was not content just to teach, but practiced it in his own flesh, asking God his Father to forgive those who obstructed him and put him to death (Luke 23:34). He awakens in us this potential for new and unexpected relationship, and makes us capable of putting an end to the terrible process of answering evil with evil, this process that shuts us in to our failings.

In order to experience forgiveness in an authentic way, we will be led to "dig" inside, reaching the center of our heart as well as the depths of our existential reality, deep into our psyche. The great temptation and principal hurdle is to skip stages, to try to get things sorted out quickly, or to run away by minimizing the difficulties. Often we reduce the process of forgiveness, making it superficial; the process is aborted and the fruit of moving out of death into life is not there. With forgiveness, we recover the idea of true love, the love which is expressed in truth.

We must dare to stay through the crisis, through the maturing, going forward step by step, getting to the bottom of our feelings, to a full conversion as we face up to ourselves.

We only approach forgiveness towards the end of the process of evangelizing the depths because we are unable to recognize immediately, in what we have done with our wounds, the ways we may, voluntarily or involuntarily, have transgressed the foundational laws of life as given by God. Similarly, we are unable to forgive with our whole being those who have hurt us until we have seen our past in the light of the Spirit and have understood that it does not enclose us in some determining and crippling way; instead, in God's grace, we can make something of it.

Every case of forgiveness being extended or received is a Passover,[6] a passage out of death into life.

---

6. Fr. *une Pâque*. Pâque refers to the Passover, meaning "passage."

13

RECEIVING FORGIVENESS

From the outset of this whole process we are involved in conversion, repentance in the most dynamic sense, which is to say, a change in direction. Many people ask why, suddenly, there is a need for this specific stage of asking and receiving forgiveness from God, why this specific step.

We can be so happy to have understood the connection between the psychological and spiritual planes that we then completely forget the idea of transgression, of sin, and not think there is any need for God's forgiveness. We may have taken on board the liberating power of the word of God and then ask: "Why, when we have poured our hearts out in truth and in prayer with the help of inner healing and group work, why now do we have to start asking for forgiveness?" The question is asked because we have perhaps not realized that seeking and receiving pardon have been prepared for by all that has gone before and are really the objective.

We arrive at a different perception of God and, as a result, of ourselves. The time when we receive forgiveness is when we, in some form, are definitively freed from any fear of God because we experience the mercy that comes to meet us in our disorder and distortions. It is forgiveness that marks a new beginning. It is a powerful medicine, and brings a real reordering; it is the time when our heart finds peace and reconciliation with our past. Whatever acts we may have committed in the past or present, it is all forgiven if we open them up to mercy. This is the time that we understand who God is, a time of wonderment.

EVANGELIZING THE DEPTHS

WOUNDING, TRANSGRESSION, SIN

A wound is neither a sin nor a transgression. If we are wounded, before anything else we are victims. Nevertheless, when we haul into the light the way in which we have reacted to our past, we become aware that we have spent most of our time transgressing the fundamental laws of life. The transgression may be involuntary or voluntary. When we have taken wrong directions through ignorance, through error, with a view to escaping unbearable pain, this is not a question of sin since sin supposes the involvement of an enlightened will.

However, the transgression may have been voluntary, and we then enter the realm of sin. "When I was seven I took such and such a direction, and I knew it was wrong," or, "I simply defied God," or, "In wanting to be all-powerful, I haughtily ignored God's laws." Others of us may have committed acts the gravity of which we are unable to minimize, knowing deep down that we cannot ignore our transgression.

To sin, in the Hebrew language, means to have the wrong aim, to miss the mark. Sin touches our relationship with God. It is a refusal to receive his life and all that truly builds us up; it is therefore a regression, a de-creation.[1] Sin is a conscious act; but for the most part, the human person is incredibly complacent about his or her sins and unaware of their fundamental sinfulness; and on top of that, the term "sin" itself is charged with confusions and bad memories. The Word of God, however, cannot imprison us into a rigid structure, nor a pattern of condemnation. It can only be a point of departure, a source of life and freedom. *Behold the Lamb of God who takes away the sins of the world*, said John the Baptist as he pointed to Jesus (John 1:29).

In its opening pages the Bible reveals how humanity deviated from God's design and entered the fundamental, initial, original sin. Adam and Eve represent man and woman, and the account of their transgression raises basic questions about the origin of evil, the nature of temptation, and the meaning of life and death. "We are dealing here with an account of a quasi mythical nature (in the best sense of the word), which does not pretend to describe an actual historical event"[2] but does give an essential, basic teaching whose meaning we need to understand. Adam and Eve show us what becomes of humanity when it wishes to become God without God,

---

1. Thévenot, *Le Péché, que peut-on en dire?* 72.
2. Thévenot, *Le Péché, que peut-on en dire?* 26.

136

without receiving its being from God and refuses its own limitations and the working of the Spirit within.

From the moment of this rupture, this fundamental division, humanity began to fall apart internally. There is no longer any unity among the three components of the personality; the three levels, the psychological, spiritual and biological, become mixed or dislocated; we become disordered. Relationship with self, with others, with the world is falsified, and the human being can now only dry up and shrivel; it will know pain and power struggles (Gen 3:14–19). It creates its own misery, suffering, and lostness. The woes that result from transgression are not sent by God: "He does no more than predict and describe."[3]

Each person relives on their own account something of the experience of Adam and Eve. We are born, moreover, in a society and world that is fallen and marred by evil through the transgressions and sin of all those that have gone before. The way back to God takes on its full meaning at this point: Jesus Christ lived fully what Adam and Eve were unable to accomplish. He shows how to be a son or daughter, become fully human, animated by the Spirit of God.

We are victims when it comes to the wounding, but we engage with sin voluntarily. It is essential to distinguish between being lost, the result of having involuntarily mistaken the route and the goal, and sin which is a voluntary straying, both chosen and nurtured.[4] The wrong directions taken following the infection of wounds are a transgression against the laws of life, but not necessarily of the same order as sin. However, sin, which supposes knowledge and the engagement of the will, is always a transgression of these laws. We always bear some responsibility and complicity in what we have done over time with the wounds, for the way in which they become infected. We are therefore never shut in in a deterministic way. Our freedom is real even if it is not total; we can always choose life by renouncing the involuntary transgression or the sin.

Seeking forgiveness, yes, but for what?

We must not lose ourselves in the endless introspection that leads to turning inwards pathologically; we have to accept a degree of uncertainty as to whether our transgression was voluntary or not. If we have lived for ten,

3. Larchet, *Thérapeutique des maladies spirituelles*, 52.
4. Xavier Thévenot, oral teaching.

twenty, or thirty years in conflict with a true direction in life, we regret with our whole being having transgressed. There is no need for us to be perfectly clear about everything before entering the process of forgiveness and reconciliation of which, whatever the case, we are so much in need.

The essential thing is to have determined to quit the transgression, whether it was voluntary or not, to renounce our complicity and to start on that pathway of repentance, which means a change of direction. This is the grace we experience as we ask and receive forgiveness from God. The seed of resurrection is then truly planted within us.

We have also to renounce whatever form of complicity may have been ours and which we often have trouble recognizing.

But as the past begins to make sense and the fear of ourselves and of God diminishes, we allow the light of the Spirit to make everything clear, and we become able to embrace this aspect of truth. It is for each of us to understand how and why we became complicit in whatever happened.

Once we have named our wrong paths for what they are, the time has come to more precisely name the transgressions our ways have led to. The issue here is transgressions of the laws of life as given by God, as well as the ways in which we have put obstacles in the way of receiving life from him. We must look again at the wrong paths and ask ourselves, "What law of life have I transgressed, choosing death rather than life?"

This is not a step that is taken as a form of intellectual reflection, but as a time of silence, of prayer; we need to take time and allow ourselves to be led by the Spirit. This is a simple but vibrant form of contemplating the Trinitarian God.[5] Our relationship with the Father will affect the way we are as sons and daughters of God (the inability to receive love, our desire for power . . .), our obedience to the laws of life, all the forms of idolatry. Relationship with the Son has to do with our relationship with others, the reality of the incarnation, the vital necessity of fully embracing the human condition by becoming consciously the temple of the living God. Relationship with the Spirit begins with the potential to let him loose within us, letting him fulfill his function, living in close and real collaboration with him and then choosing whether to shut ourselves in or open up to him, whether to experience the tomb or the resurrection, immobility or creativity.

5. Thévenot, *Compter sur Dieu*, 113–114.

THE TIME FOR FORGIVENESS

The moment we receive God's forgiveness is unique, an intimate, foundational moment in our journey. Receiving forgiveness is a definite, conscious act of great depth and it causes the heart to melt. It leads to a deep sense of detachment after what has often been a painful pathway; the prodigal son had to eat dust before losing his illusions about himself. God's pardon is offered totally freely, whatever our condition, whoever we are, if we come back to him in a complete change of heart.

Again, the forgiveness offered has to be received, and numerous obstacles to receiving this gift need to be recognized. That the gift is free does not therefore allow of inertia, passivity, or a lack of responsibility on our part; we are thoroughly implicated in receiving it. Many a person fails to receive forgiveness as a result of an incapacity to believe themselves loved while they see themselves as unworthy.

How many there are who live under a load of remorse, of guilt, or shame! How many fail to internalize the pardon granted, and go on thinking that they can never be totally washed and rid of the burdens of the past or present! How often too, like the elder son in the parable, they have a hard heart and think there is no need of pardon and have nothing with which to reproach themselves. They then pass the gift and the abundance by, depriving themselves of the fatted calf for a feast.

When we return to God, we are immediately forgiven. It is done. We then have to step out in faith; without awaiting any feelings, we have to forcefully remind ourselves, whenever doubt menaces, that we are truly forgiven. This is not a matter of receiving a little bit of forgiveness[6] for a short time, but of taking hold of it, appropriating it fully, of experiencing what Jesus announced, that what was lost is saved, and so life is recovered. Such a time is one of great joy, as much for the one who forgives as it is for the one forgiven (Luke 15:23–24).

We often say that we are unable to forgive ourselves

This is a wrong way of looking at things; only God forgives. It is not for us to forgive ourselves. It would be more correct to say that we are unable to receive the forgiveness of God for ourselves. If that is how we put it, things are already clearer. There is no way that we should stay in this condition of

6. François Varillon, oral teaching.

refusing God's gift, so we absolutely have to ask the Spirit to show us why we are doing it. Often, what we have here is a power grasping behavior, now camouflaged behind a false humility.

"No one could ever forgive me; what I have done is too serious, so I am quite unworthy of receiving pardon." Thus do we deny love, thinking that our wrongdoing is more powerful than the love of God. Others condemn and accuse themselves as they attempt to sort out their problems on their own: they self-punish, as did Judas. Others again will not admit the idea that they might fall back, and so cannot forgive themselves for their setbacks or limitations. If they had perfectionist parents, they might feel obliged to perform, to surpass others, if they are to survive. If they have been admired unconditionally or idolized, they may not be able to allow themselves even the slightest shortcoming. Sometimes there are those who are bound by a prohibition, that they not disappoint one or other of their parents who was counting on them to achieve what they had not managed. They then cannot forgive themselves for not having fulfilled this need. Many become filled with resentment when they are unable to accept what they have been, the wrong way in which they have built their lives, or allowed them to be built.

Very often, the anger we hold against some person who has done us wrong is really anger against ourselves: how could we have been blind for so long? We need to be aware of this displaced violence and accept deep down the nature of our past behavior, what we have been; it is after all the truth. Some people fall into a sort of despair when they discover they have gone wrong; they think that all they have been through is of no value, totally forgetting the long and necessary road that is purification. The Father has been loving and has sought us throughout our past. He has been working through us, through the tares and the good seed. Nothing will ever be totally pure, but equally, nothing we have been through is lost. If the events of today have been possible, it is because the past has prepared us for it.

Guilt[7]

Guilt is a complex subject that touches on deeply rooted feelings of fear, as well as wrong ideas about God, about punishment, about expiation . . . .

A lasting sense of guilt engages our energies, and at the same time holds us back from new awakenings of conscience. We have to make a

7. Thévenot, *Les Péchés, que peut-on en dire?* 51–53.

distinction between objective guilt and a subjective, diffuse feeling of guilt, and then look our experience in the face—is the sense of guilt well founded or not? From the standpoint of a believer, it is preferable to replace the term "guilt" with sinner. There is, indeed, a fundamental difference between being guilty and being a sinner.

Guilt pertains to the level of the psyche. "It is an internal reality of the mind (psyche), affecting the conscience, that then feels crushed by a weight, standing before an internal tribunal that is ready to judge and then impose punishment."[8] A part of ourselves accuses, condemns, and leads us to self-punishment. Guilt is experienced as a closed circuit. Round and round we go, shut in on ourselves in remorse. The recognition of sin and repentance, however, is between God and us; we are immediately on another level, in a different dimension, one that supposes that we are bound to God and know the laws of life. The issue then becomes the change from being a sinner to a sinner forgiven by God, like the woman who poured perfume over Jesus' feet (Luke 7:36–50), the adulterous woman (John 8:1–11), the good thief (Luke 23:39–43), and so many others in the Gospels. Jesus said, *I do not condemn you. Go, and sin no more* (John 8:11). There is no need to pay, to expiate (though if possible there should be reparation for any consequences to our actions); just returning to Christ, to the Father.

Guilt is tied to our expectations of ourselves, and to what we think others' expectations of us are. Here we find again our quest to fulfill the idealized image we have of self, and on that basis proceed to the mistaken, negative view we can take of ourselves. Our "inner judge" leads us on into permanent self-accusation for not matching up.

The feeling of guilt can be general and diffuse, as well as permanent and without apparent cause: nevertheless it is a sign that something within us is not clear. It can result from a state of real but unrecognized sin, for example adultery, complete rejection of parents, denial of our birth origin, hidden rivalry, longstanding bitterness, disrespect, unacknowledged hatred, etc. We have to name our sin clearly, own it, confess it, cease to justify ourselves, and ask for forgiveness.

Thérèse had cared attentively for her sick mother, but was absent at the time of her death. She reproached herself bitterly and eventually was engulfed by a crushing sense of remorse. In fact, when we spoke, she realized that she had been harboring a stubborn sense of bitterness towards her mother, really a sort of murderous and deeply hidden hatred. Her mother

8. Thévenot, *Les Péchés, que peut-on en dire?* 51.

had always run down her own husband and they had divorced; Thérèse in fact accused her of being responsible for the rupture with her father. She needed to review, in the Spirit, this part of her past and name the sin that had taken up residence within her.

Joel had lived in a permanent state of guilt for many years; he felt thoroughly unworthy. He said that he enjoyed a deep friendship with a woman other than his wife in a spiritual communion in which he found great fulfillment. He had reached the point of no longer having any communication with his spouse. He recognized that he was living for this interchange with the friend, but he nevertheless continued to justify the relationship. In reality this was a form of adultery in disguise. He was not in the light about this, and it was the principal source of his sense of guilt.

The fact of trivializing acts that concern life and death (abortion for example) can open the door to a latent sense of guilt that we are unable to account for or name. Similarly, we may choose to simply justify without nuance sexual deviances and fantasies (which are often in reality disordered behaviors with an origin in blockages or some fixation in our emotional development). We may entertain a certain complacency about taking refuge in the imaginary, in dreams, about frittering away time, squandering energy which should be devoted to the present, forgetting what is really important. This easy-going complacency can lead to feelings of guilt if the disorder is not named. Many people say that they are ready to quit their deviances but are not prepared to renounce the secondary benefits they gain, which is to say, to lose the pleasure they secure, and accept that they will no longer demand attention . . . .

Guilt can become entrenched because we live in fear of accusation. We can feel responsible to have caused some accident for which we have no real responsibility at all: the sickness or death of a mother during pregnancy or at birth, an accident to a brother or sister . . . . The fact of being a boy or a girl when the other sex was wanted may be a cause, as too may be just existing if we arrived at a bad moment so that we either were or felt that we were unwanted . . . .

We have to watch not to feel guilt mistakenly. This can indeed happen through a lack of discernment (unjust accusations from others, children who are victims of sexual abuse . . .). It is certainly just as serious to lose one's grounding and become confused as it is to be unable to question oneself.

Seeking an ill-conceived ideal can also be the source of false guilt.

Anne married a widower with three children and, from the moment of their marriage, experienced a permanent sense of guilt. After many very difficult years, she realized that she had settled on the role of the perfect, ideal step-mother. In reality, she was not accepting her own limitations or those of her step children. Healing took place through refusing this misplaced guilt: love was not what she thought.

Finally, we must realize that we have a duty not to obey a desire or request that is not of the Spirit and does not conform to the laws of life. We are not to be complicit in anything wrong or allow ourselves to be upset by unjustified reproaches.

Reparation

It is right, good, and normal to make reparation, if possible, for any wrong done to another. In the Gospel, Zacchaeus, the rich tax-collector, in a flash, simply because Jesus had invited himself to dine at his house so that he now found himself before the very person of integrity, was suddenly aware of his condition as a cheat. He decided to give half his goods to the poor and return fourfold to anyone he had defrauded.

Along the way, some of us become aware of the wrong we may have done others, often unwittingly. This can be a great cause of pain, notably for many parents, and it is not always possible to make up for the damage our actions have done. This is a limitation we have to accept (Luke 23:42). Nevertheless, we can ask the Spirit to inspire inner actions that in some way can move what has been harmed back towards life. We can, for example, recognize the existence and importance of a family member, be accepting of their hurt, and re-establish a relationship that may be unseen but very real. In the case of abortion, for example, we can recognize and name the child that did not live. . . . Here we are discussing forms of reparation that are known to ourselves alone, but we can be sure that there will be something repaired invisibly even though we may not see any external fruit. The good thief made a form of reparation for his entire life by totally yielding his heart, in his humble, trusting plea.

It is not always possible to expressly ask forgiveness from others; this is simply at times not opportune. But we can be sure that when we internally make a request for forgiveness from God and the other party (even if they have died), a knot is being in some way unraveled.

CONFUSIONS

All too often we call sin something that is not sin, and we don't see our own sin. We are blind but believe that we see clearly (John 9:40–41). Our eye is not good (Luke 11:34). The prophet Isaiah cries out about this perversion of sight: *Woe to you who call good evil and evil good, who make the dark light and the light darkness* (Isa 5:20).

For the most part *we call that which is good evil* because of our wrong ideas about God. A mistake or failure is not a sin. We certainly have to look carefully at what our part might have been in a given situation, but mistakes are not to be put on the level of sin. Temptation is not sin; Christ was tempted, as are we all, each in his or her own way. Sin is falling in with the temptation. The fact that we have limitations is not sin—it is the human condition. Being troubled is not sin, but there are those who find this hard to accept and thereby add to their trouble, when again trouble is a part of our normal human limitations; it is impossible to avoid being upset by people or situations. The issue is how to manage difficulties by living in the light and strength of the Spirit. Being unable to accept the reality of being troubled is another manifestation of our will to omnipotence.[9] Of course, a wound is not a sin, but it can become the cause of transgression or sin to the degree in which we don't know how to deal with it. Being in a state of crisis is not a sin. We must learn to experience crisis abiding in the presence of God, without being alarmed and without wishing to shorten the necessary time for the crisis to play out.

Spiritual battles do not constitute sin; they are a normal element in the life of every child of God. Anyone who has chosen to live as a son or daughter of God will not go forward without the spiritual warfare that gives rise to fruitfulness and growth. A spiritual battle is not a crisis. The two conditions are not on the same level. Spiritual warfare is when a person is participating consciously and actively, on a daily basis, in the work of God in them, faithful to the choices they have made.

Accepting our first responses to something is not a sin. On the contrary, they are a precious source of information. To recognize our violence, our hatred, our rebellion, taking the time to investigate—this is not sin. Allowing oneself the right to suffer, to see some sorrow through to the end, is not sin. How often we accuse ourselves of lacking faith when seeing the pain through to its conclusion in God's presence is a condition of life.

9. Thévenot, *Repères éthiques pour un monde nouveau*, 49.

Listening to the voice of the body or the soul is not sin. We must recognize and accept any burnout, a lowering of the nervous or physical state, and not allow ourselves to be eaten alive by others. The Sabbath has a deep, vital, spiritual meaning and is not optional in our lives: *Come apart into a desert place and rest for a while* (Mark 6:31), said Jesus to his disciples. A period of depression following a serious shock of whatever sort is part of life. We have to take time out for such an event without blaming ourselves.

Wishing to live in full liberty, rightly understood, is not a sin. It is important to learn to go through the necessary separations; we are not to submit to manipulative behavior, power trips, domination, or emotional blackmail. We are not to let ourselves be destroyed. Contrary to what we may believe, sin may consist in not developing the freedom we are all given as a seed, a potential, a capacity for growth.

The liberty of the child of God is real. It is not anarchical because it has direction. It is the capacity to live life allowing the inspiration of the Spirit. *The truth will make you free people* (John 8:32); *where the Spirit of the Lord is, there is freedom* (2 Cor 3:17). Becoming free with this liberty requires discernment and clear understanding. In short, daring to be oneself, recognizing and developing one's uniqueness, is not sin if there is an awareness in relationship of respect for the uniqueness of others.

Calling that which is bad good. If this is the case, we have lost our bearings. Frequently the very idea of sin or transgression is non-existent, totally erased. Everything is psychologized; it all becomes excusable because we have suffered. We no longer have within us the criteria to distinguish between right and wrong; anything goes as long as I am fulfilled and my needs and desires are being met. We then justify every transgression, every disorder on the pretext of tolerance. Everything we experience is the fault of others, of our parents, of our past. We accord ourselves the status of victims without discerning our part.

We might regard as good the perfectionism that is really a refusal to accept limitations. The demands of this wear us down and keep us in the place of omnipotence, in illusion, or in legalism. We might regard as good, behaviors which are self-destructive or self-punishing, along with our ways of making false sacrifices and unrequired acts of reparation. We might see to as generosity what is in fact a flight into activism, a wrong attempt to forget self. We can also be burying our talents out of false humility, through fear of pride, fear of success, or fear of becoming rich.

All these behaviors and many more besides can have an appearance of good but are in reality bad, ways that lead to death.

14

FORGIVING

It is not possible to forgive when it is too early, nor can we afford to forgive too quickly, whether the event is past or present. Forgiving those who have acted badly towards us, remitting their debt, "letting go of whatever has done us ill,"[1] which is another facet of forgiveness, all this involves a deep detachment that can only take place in stages. As long as we have not gone over our past in all its fullness and are blind, broken down or mixed up, we cannot really forgive. Not until we no longer consider ourselves solely as victims, have become fully aware of the ways of death we have chosen and decided to abandon them for the ways of life, have set our hand to the plow and begun to recover our true identity—not until then is it possible to forgive.

This time does, however, arrive, and it is absolutely of the essence! It is the culmination of the conversion process, the season of blessing and liberation. God is the source of forgiveness, so it is only ever in his grace that we can forgive. This stage is quite impossible in our own strength, but we are nonetheless implicated in the process.

ACKNOWLEDGING THE ILL

The first essential step, prior to any act of forgiveness, is full awareness of the wrong suffered. If we don't realize the extent of the pain, of the violence that has taken root in us, it will not be possible to experience forgiveness in

1. Basset, *Le pardon originel*, 422.

its fullness. If all our emotions are rubbed out, denied, how are we to know what and who we are to pardon? It is with the starting point of sorrow and rebellion that forgiveness is to take place. If we deny them, the act of forgiveness will not produce its fruit of transformation, of moving out of death into life.

We have already looked at the resistance we have to face in this process. However, there are many who try to forgive without the process. In seeking to forget (but forgiving is not forgetting) or to excuse (and neither is forgiving excusing), they fail to get to the bottom of things, or perhaps take refuge in the mental, in the intellect, so as not to be confronted by painful new considerations. Many think that the remembering of an offence is an indication that they have not forgiven, but it is not possible to forget an event that has done us harm. The memory is stored away in the mind, while forgiveness is a matter of the deep will. They are not the same thing. "The resurrection was not the forgetting of the passion." "Christ was raised with his scars, and we too retain within us the scars of our past, but they are not signs of despondency or condemnation, but of healing and salvation."[2]

God's forgiveness does not draw a veil over our past, nor does it make it void. No, it allows of a reconciliation with the past and its integration into the present. The sign that the forgiveness is really alive in us and that it has been fully given and received is that, while the memory is still there, it is no longer destructive and no longer prevents us living.

Daring to look full in the face how much we have been hurt in the course of the past is a little different from simply acknowledging the ill done us, but it is part of it.

The second step is definitive acceptance of the reality undergone and the wrong done us. We must not deny it or minimize it; we can't change it. This acceptance is a very deep aspect of conversion, an essential stage.

Finally, we must not forget the possibility that we will react to an event that reopens one of our wounds, bringing the same pain we have previously felt. We then find ourselves again unable to forgive. However, we will have grown in Christ and so can pass through a difficulty like this in the grace and presence of God and accept it in the strength the Spirit gives us.

2. Mgr. Lustiger in a talk on German radio a few days before the 87th *Katholikentag* in Dusseldorf.

FORGIVING

SEEING THINGS CORRECTLY

Our responsibility

Without realizing it some people can refuse or become unable to see their responsibility. Then, little by little, they persuade themselves of their own good conscience. Being able to examine yourself is nevertheless a fundamental disposition of heart in receiving the kingdom. *Do not harden your heart*, says the scripture (Ps 94:8). *I have come to give sight to the blind*, says Jesus, and your sin is not being blind but believing that you see (John 9:41), to *have eyes but see nothing* (Mark 8:18).

Neither, though, do we have to believe ourselves systematically responsible for all that happens. It's essential that we leave behind our confusion and sort out what is and is not right in the words and behavior of others. By working together with the Spirit we can manage this and be assured in our hearts.

Wrong relationships

Relationships can be wrong, notably when we are looking to someone else to meet our needs.

If this is the case we are liable to become frustrated if we don't obtain what we want and then reject the other person, all of which can be a further obstacle to forgiveness. For example, if we believe that the other person will serve as father or mother, bringing us security, providing or confirming our identity, we will not be able to forgive them if they don't perform. As we learn to form our identity in Christ, we can leave others with the choice to love us in their own way or not love us at all.

Demanding that others change in line with our views can be a serious obstacle to forgiveness. The danger is of not forgiving the way they deal with the residual effects of their past and with their suffering, not forgiving the way they actually are. If we see this difference as an opposition to our wishes, we will be permanently frustrated by an unrealized expectation; if we feel threatened by another way of thinking, of living, of communicating—we will not be able to forgive.

EVANGELIZING THE DEPTHS

Pursuing the ideal

The idea of the ideal, whether it has to do with our picture of marriage, family, children, community, . . . can lead us straight into a trap. We all have ideals, and this is good, but we have to guard against making them absolute, a goal in themselves, since we are then liable to fall into legalism or some utopian dream. . . . People do become completely fused with their ideal, and then risk passing their whole life seeking to bring it to pass and exist for that purpose only. If, for example, we carry around an idealized picture of marriage, we won't be able to forgive our partner for being the principal obstacle to its realization. We then put an unbearable burden on them.

Thérèse was married. At the time of their marriage she and her husband enjoyed great oneness. From one year to the next, Thérèse became more and more involved in the spiritual life, while her husband went his way—he had a simple way of relating to things, to the earth, to the material world. He was very clever with his hands, and expressed his love for Thérèse by making things easy for her materially. She, however, became fixed on a very specific goal—to have a deep communion with her husband on a metaphysical level. Her demands became such that their relationship was in danger; she had forged an ideal for the marriage. Their relationship was only restored the day Thérèse understood that she had to kiss her ideal good-bye. She could then forgive her husband for being what he was—different from her—and pursue other options in life.

Similarly, if we expect our children to take a direction that conforms to our ideal, it will prove difficult to forgive them if they follow a different path.

A lot of people think that an ideal communal life is one in which no conflict ever breaks out, so anything that could give rise to confrontation is disregarded. Differences can only then be felt as contrary: there is no real dialogue and internal violence becomes a settled fact. It becomes very difficult to forgive those who originate conflicts and destroy the ideal. Moreover, any forgiveness is likely to be superficial because glossing over difference is a sure way to kill life.

Others

Stop judging by appearances (John 7:24). *Do not set yourself up as judges and you will not be judged. Do not condemn and you will not be condemned* (Luke 6:37). How are we to understand these words of Christ?

No one is to judge or condemn anyone. Judgment belongs to the Father. Nevertheless, for us, it is important, necessary, to be able to discern the appropriateness and quality of some action, to be objective in our analysis of a situation; while we have never to condemn anyone, we do have to vigorously reject behaviors that are not of the Spirit. We don't wish to engage in truncated forms of forgiveness which hold us in a state of inner conflict and division.

Renouncing judgment of an "offender"

This is a command we are given, as though to underline the vital importance of this issue. Not judging others means that we are not going to seek to evaluate their degree of culpability, the bad stuff they might have in their heart, nor to dissect their motives and intentions. "At the heart of forgiveness, as at the heart of the garden of Eden [. . .], there is a renunciation of 'knowing' evil in the way that God knows things, all things. [. . .] Forgiveness is rooted in the tree of life and not in the tree of the knowledge of good and evil."[3] God alone knows what is going on in a human heart; we have no way of knowing its wounds. This is most probably the reason why the prohibition on judging is so radical, so imperative, that Jesus himself asked the Father to forgive his executioners, as though he himself did not recognize any right to judge; only the Father knew the truth of their culpability.

Not reducing a person to their actions

Many people tend to confine their view of others solely to their behavior. Without realizing it, one thing leads to another and a point is reached of entirely overlooking the other person, not listening to them or attaching weight to anything they think or say. This is a form of murder. It then becomes impossible to forgive.

We are not to isolate, confine a person to one moment in their life, the one when they hurt us. Real though our prejudice against them might be, by our attitude towards them we are witnesses that they are and remain a child of God, as unique as ourselves and loved by the *Father of all* (Eph 4:6) who watches over them. A person is not what they have done, they can change. This is precisely the significance of the father of the prodigal, waiting in the roadway, believing in the possible return of his son, in a turnaround of his

3. Basset, *Le pardon originel*, 447.

heart. This waiting of his meant that the son could understand that he was still "lovable," and this attitude was the seed of healing in the son's heart, the son who thought himself so vile (Luke 15:20). "The truest looks of love are those which wait expectantly for us."[4]

Discerning the actions and behavior of the offender

This indeed is part of our responsibility. We should not be accepting of actions that are not founded in the Spirit or do not conform to the laws of life; neither should we become complicit in wrongdoing.

We can name "what it is that has done us wrong"[5] without condemning the person by whom we have been hurt. Many people have a strong resistance to the act of forgiveness because they believe that forgiveness involves an acceptance of the other person's behavior, which is something they don't wish. "Do not be mistaken about the enemy," said Gandhi, "the enemy is not the English; it is the law."

Forgiveness does not mean excusing; there are acts that are simply inexcusable. To systematically excuse under a pretext of charity is one way of denying the other person liberty. Forgiving does not mean accepting, and neither does it do away with confronting. If we don't bow to another person's desire when it is contrary to the laws of life, we are indeed likely to have some conflict, but we have to take this on board in the light and the power of the Spirit, in truth and with full respect for the other, without aggression, vengeance, or contempt. We understand here how we could in the past have refused conditions that were imposed on us, and done so without falling into judgment or condemnation.

In her book, *Crisis in Masculinity*, Leanne Payne gives a very clear example of a proper exercise of forgiveness.[6] This concerned a homosexual man who was addressing (inwardly) his father. His prayer could be summarized in this way: "This is the great wrong your behavior caused me [he names it precisely]. For all this wrong, I forgive you, I remit your debt to me, I make no demand for you to change, but neither will I ever submit to your wishes or your will in so far as they are not of the Spirit and do not conform to the laws of life."

---

4. P. Baudiquey on *The Prodigal Son* by Rembrandt.

5. Basset, *Le pardon originel*, 422.

6. Payne, *Crisis in Masculinity*, 73–74.

It is impossible for us to forgive unless we vigorously say no to anything asked of or imposed on us that is not of the Spirit.

INTERNAL CONDITIONS CONTRARY TO FORGIVENESS

Contempt for others

We must first question ourselves as to whether we harbor feelings of contempt for others.

Jacques' father had been an extremely weak man who had given in to his wife and his mother-in-law, and the atmosphere of the family home was poisonous. Jacques became aware of the contempt he felt for his father and, similarly, for any man he thought to be weak and fragile. This root, which had been planted in him through his relationship with his father, was always there.

It is very important to look at whom we might have felt contempt for or still feel that way towards. This particular area can be very surprising—the behavior is so very frequent.

Christ never felt this contempt or disdain for anyone at all; it was a feeling unknown to him. It was precisely this absence that drew around him the crowd of people who knew themselves to be at fault and believed themselves unclean. Jesus spoke to them of the kingdom, announcing the gospel to them, and inviting them to follow him. He behaved so as to reveal to them their value. He touched them, let them touch him, ate with them. It is so wonderful to be welcomed for who we are; in itself this is a profound healing.[7] Jesus was this way with everyone, with the Samaritan woman who belonged to a group disdained by the Jews, and whose emotional life was a complete mess (John 4:1–28), with the unclean woman who was losing blood yet dared to touch him (Matt 9:21), or with Nicodemus, the Pharisee, who dared not meet Jesus in daylight and came by night (John 3:1–21).

We may even feel contempt for ourselves, forgetful or ignorant that we are created in the image of God.

We asked André during a session where he felt he was in the parable of the prodigal son. "Me? I am tending the pigs; I couldn't be anywhere else." The turnaround in his heart came when he understood that his place was not watching pigs but in the arms of the Father, and that this could be his experience without delay, immediately, just as he was.

7. Leclerc, *Le Royaume caché*, 81–105.

Contempt for others could focus on any particular point, according to who we are, our past, our ideals, our successes, our failures. We might feel this way towards one or other of our parents, a member of our family, an institution, a race, a social class, the poor or the rich, intellectuals or laborers, a church, ... If we have contempt towards anyone, then we have not truly forgiven.

Resentment

It is possible that we have in us longstanding and deeply buried resentment; this is a real poison that eats away at the soul. Acknowledging the resentment is the first step; it can often be enough just to be faced with the word to be instantly clear on this issue.

Many of us are often very complacent in relation to resentment when it is an attitude opposed to forgiveness, leading as it does to holding on indefinitely to the wrong in others, fixing, paralyzing, binding, instead of letting go, releasing, untying. The old becomes solidly rooted and the new cannot supervene. *Let the dead bury their dead* (Matt 8:22). *If someone nourishes anger in their heart, how can they then ask the Lord for healing?* (Sirach 28:3).[8] The Spirit cannot work freely in a conflicted, discordant situation if we are enmeshed in resentment.

So, let us take time to open up to the light of the Spirit the causes of this resentment and then expel it from our heart.

Revenge

Resentment can lead on to feelings of revenge. Revenge, says Daniel Sibony, is "a debt stored up in the memory, an established need waiting to be put into action."[9] Wishing to be avenged is a desire for something bad for someone else, so it is the opposite of blessing; it is to rejoice in their fall, in their misery: "Serves him right!" The desire for revenge is most often born of a sense of powerlessness before some evil that has been done to us; it is the only way out we can find and is profoundly destructive. It is also a refusal to accept the past.

8 Or Ecclesiasticus. "If a man bears a grudge . . ." Knox translation.

9. Sibony, "Pour une éthique de l'être," 333.

There are a thousand ways to be avenged: pushing oneself to be successful, to prove one's worth against all odds—"you'll see what I can do"; self-destruction, to show others how unhappy they have made us; refusing to live and be healed, since it would be too easy to just wipe the slate clean as if we had not suffered; blaming the other party, denying their worth.

A murderous clarity

Some of us are very quick to see the faults in others. As quick as a flash, we seize on some twist or another. What are we to do about this?[10]

The way we see needs to be purified, converted, as do all our senses and faculties. If our perception is not converted it will lead to judging and condemning. The other person is then shut in to the labels we feel appropriate; we know better than them what they should be thinking, saying, and doing. This attitude imprisons, enchains instead of liberating. It then becomes easy to slip into a very destructive form of intelligent malice, which is one of the shapes taken by the "omnipotent" self. However, neither can we simply erase what we perceive as being correct and, under the pretext of being respectful, try to please the other person.

Christ told us what to do about our attitude, our "eye." First of all it has to be just—our judgment has to be correct; we have a tendency to maximize the wrong we see in others and minimize our own faults. Here we have the story of the speck we see in our neighbor's eye when there is a plank in our own (Luke 6:41). The way we see needs to be at the disposal of the Spirit, which is to say, light and truth, but the loving truth, which is given to help and to bring growth, patient truth.

The first step is to commit what we have seen to the heart of Christ: it is the Father's affair, not ours. *You, Lord, you know the hearts of all* (Acts 1:24). This form of inner fasting leads us out of the grip that we exercise over another when we dissect them in this way. With this same change we also put ourselves in the position of a servant of the Spirit by making ourselves available to him in the way he indicates, as a helper, an instrument in the relationship. We need to be ready to speak if a door opens. If that happens, we allow a period of silence to pray about the words to speak and the

---

10. The discussion here is solely about forgiveness, not counselling, which the author points out is a different situation, in which someone comes looking for specific help and there is a need for discernment; different rules therefore apply, and thorough training is necessary.

correct time for them. If this is the way we act, we are uncluttering the path and giving the Spirit free rein to change our attitude. This inner withdrawal or fasting gives time and space for the new. We must give place to Christ and set our thoughts at rest, a Sabbath rest. Whenever a destructive thought recurs, we present it to the Spirit and replace it with a word of life. We can count on the grace of God, who is alongside us in the fast.

We also need to be ready to hold our tongue; our disposition towards keeping quiet is a good indication as to whether or not we are living in the Spirit. Our tongue, which can be full of "a deadly poison" (Jas 3:8), needs converting too, to be submitted. There is no need to spread abroad what we have seen in others under the pretext of telling the truth.

Jesus, with all the knowledge he had of people, never put restrictions on anyone; neither, though, did he ever pull back from what he needed to say or do. We must ask him to introduce us to a full understanding of his behavior, helping us to know how to live. In numerous episodes in the Gospels, Jesus "passed by," "withdrew," and went elsewhere when attacked (John 4:3). Nevertheless, he confronted his trial and his death full on; he did not pass this by; but here too we find him not responding to Pilate's question, *"What is truth?"* (John 18:38). His silence turned the question back on its speaker and his choices. As we live in the Spirit, we learn to discern when to answer and when to be quiet, to pass by.

LOVE YOUR ENEMIES AND PRAY FOR THOSE WHO PERSECUTE YOU

If you love those who love you [. . .] *and if you greet only your brothers, what are you doing that is other than normal?* (Matt 5:44)

These words would seem impossible to practice when some relationship is marred or even broken, when the enemy is the source of wounds so serious they could destroy us, when we are faced with the unforgiveable. People with a particularly burdensome past but who have gone back over it in the light and love of Christ know very well that this step remains, and that, until it is taken, their path of recovery is not complete. However, we must not be precipitate in seeking to love our enemies or even to pray for them. The first thing is to understand—just what does it mean to love your enemy?

FORGIVING

To love

Christ's starting point is that we do have enemies; he was no dreamer and knew that we do not live in a perfect world with perfect harmony. He was under no illusions as to the spiritual state of some of the scribes and Pharisees, who were his brothers in faith; instead he foresaw that they would have him put to death. "A biblical man is always faced by his enemy. This is a fact that we don't so much as question, [...] it is a given in history. Sin has turned opposition into hatred."[11] Jesus experienced all this and would not have involved us in it if it was beyond our scope.

We begin by discerning clearly who the enemy is. It could be a stranger, a neighbor, a member of our family, even part of ourselves. . . . We must see that we don't label as an enemy someone who simply calls us into question and is right to do so.

Loving one's enemy and praying for them does not in any way mean that we are going to allow them to destroy us. Love is never destructive, and any act that would lead to our destruction or that of others is not founded on love. It is therefore often necessary to be firm and put boundaries in place. By praying or seeking to love an enemy in a confused manner, we risk losing our way.

Loving an enemy is not a matter of the emotions or sentiments but of the will; it is a choice born of a desire to be in full agreement with the laws of the kingdom. It means loving as Jesus loved, experiencing *agape*, the love that has its source in God and is a transforming dynamic ("transdynamizing") of God's love. The word of Christ is a commandment of life and does not bear directly on the feelings; we don't endeavor to love with natural sympathy or affection. Loving one's enemy does not mean that we have a deep interchange of views, that we trust them, or are bound together in friendship. Loving one's enemy does mean respecting the personhood of the one who does us wrong, and that we acknowledge them in their identity as children of God in their unique way.

The inner act of forgiveness towards the enemy could by expressed as, "Today, I forgive you, I remit your debt, and I commit to respecting your person." This would translate into an inner commitment not to speak ill of them, not to run them down with sharp words, while at no point becoming complicit in the wrong they have done.

11. *Vocabulaire de théologie biblique*, 356–57.

Loving the enemy means not returning blow for blow, and not, in turn, becoming an enemy to them. *My foot almost slipped, I all but stumbled; [. . .] if I had spoken it would have been to speak like them and I would have betrayed the generation of your children, [. . .] but you have taken me by my right hand and by your counsel you will lead me* (Ps 72:2, 15, 23–24). Loving one's enemy means wishing them well and not harm, recognizing the fruit they bear, the potential in what they do, but maintaining a proper sense of discernment and the necessary prudence.

What does it mean to pray for one's enemy?

We cannot pray for our enemies when we are simply confused, but it is always possible to act in a way that looses us from confusion and helps us to be correctly orientated before we pray. We will need to be loosed from the behavior of the other person, from their problem, from the power they have over us. We then free them from the wrong they have done us, from the wrong we might have done them, leaving them free to go their own way as we commit both them and ourselves into God's blessing.

It is not always wise to obstinately pray every day for our enemy; doing so can actually drive us further into difficulty. We also need to guard against being too specific in our praying for them because we can easily fall into effectively trying to settle accounts through prayer.

There is a form of intercessory prayer that can help get us into the right place, one which produces abundant fruit. It consists in allowing the presence of God to become established at the heart of the conflicted relationship, in exactly the same way as we open a door or window in the house to allow the sun in. We stay in this attitude until we have the inner absolute certainty that the presence of God is really there, at work. If the agitation comes back, we concentrate afresh on this assurance. This is one form of the prayer of praise. It is not something done on its own, and it doesn't happen of itself. It is not enough just to think that God is, and that he is at work in everything; it is not a question of turning the problem over to him as though we were just disencumbering ourselves. No, this is a different process, in which we allow Him who knocks at the door to come in. Experience shows that praying in this way leads us to suspend passing judgment on the person. Prayer becomes a form of peaceable contemplation, of total faith in the work of God.

We are to ask God to forgive our enemies, just as Jesus did at the moment of his death (Luke 23:34). The issue then, of course, was of forgiveness being given to the person of the enemy, not the blessing of their actions. This demonstrates that forgiveness comes from God, and that it passes through the heart, through the asking of the Servant who was wounded in his flesh, in that which was dearest to him. Do we really long, from the bottom of our hearts, for our enemies to be totally forgiven? When this is the case, it is a tremendously purifying force in this walk of loving our enemies. We have no need to know if the enemy will or will not receive God's pardon; we have done our part in opening the door, knowing that it is God who is able to melt any resistance.

A biblical journey

The Bible tells the story of a man who could only see in his enemy the hatred he was full of himself, but who, as he became aware of his own wounding, received forgiveness. The man is Jacob (Gen 27:1–34).

Jacob had been a cheat in his youth: he had stolen the blessing that was reserved for the elder son, Esau, and tricked his father, Isaac. Esau, enraged, sought to kill Jacob, who fled. After a highly eventful passage of time, Jacob heard the call of God: *Go back to the country of your fathers and your family, and I will be with you* (Gen 31:3). Go back to your roots, face up to your past in the light of my presence, and you will receive my blessing.[12] Jacob therefore returned to the land of his fathers, and of course, his first meeting was with his mortal enemy, Esau, the embodiment of his own trickery. At first he was overcome by fear and sought to protect himself by running away, and this led to him spending an entire night alone, battling, fighting (Gen 32:23–33). There are many possible interpretations of Jacob's struggle. One is that the whole of his past came back to him, that he could see it all in detail, and was confronted by deep-reaching doubt. He had probably lost all positive self-esteem. How could God ever bless him given his fraudulent past?[13]

This however was the route he was to embrace, and he became able to receive blessing into the core of his tortuous life (Gen 32:30). He became

12. Following Joseph Pyronnet, who proposes this re-reading of our lives with Jacob as our starting point.

13. This interpretation of Jacob's wrestling can be found in a working paper by Raphael Cohen, "Tikoun Peracha," 1991.

himself. He met God at the heart of his confused and deeply hidden reality: *You will no longer be called Jacob but Israel* (Gen 32:29). His attitude and his heart were changed completely. He had identified Esau with his own murderous hatred, and suddenly, understanding that he was welcomed, loved, and blessed through all the twistedness that he was no longer hiding, he saw Esau as a child of God. He no longer had any fear of him. *He bowed down to the ground seven times as he drew near to his brother* (Gen 33:3). This sort of prostration was reserved for God, a sign that he saw the presence of God in his brother: he acknowledged the Spirit as living in Esau. Esau was completely overcome by this greeting: *He ran to meet him, took him in his arms, threw himself on his neck and embraced him; they wept* (Gen 33:4).

The relationship was totally transformed on both sides; Jacob's attitude caused Esau's heart to melt, and he was able to abandon his hatred and pain. The story of Jacob and Esau is very precious, hitting us right where we are, and showing us the way of heart conversion. When someone becomes an enemy we can inwardly, secretly, and silently, bow down seven times before him or her, before the heart indwelt by the presence of God, before this embryonic child of God. It may prove necessary for us to repeat this act across the space of weeks or months, until we are able to know it as a physical fact.

SOME DETAILS ON FORGIVENESS

Forgiveness does not necessarily mean the end of pain. Many people think after an act of pardon they will not suffer again. This is not always the case, but the suffering will not be the same since it no longer leads to death and can be undergone with a peaceful heart. There is life there now.

Forgiveness is unconditional. It is free and excludes any bargaining. There is no question of forgiving "provided" the other person takes some step or other, that they acknowledge their errors, becoming aware of the wrong they have done. All of that is their affair, and we have no control over it.

We are not to forgive and pursue some particular outcome. We might, for example, be hoping that forgiveness will mean avoiding the grief we cannot face if there is a rupture in our marriage: "If I forgive, I will be able to explain myself completely and there can be dialogue again . . . ."

When we forgive, the relationship is not necessarily restored outwardly, although everything is there to make this possible. Complete restoration of a relationship does not depend on us alone—the other person must want it too. It is often necessary to move away, or, if this is not possible, to set some kind of inner distance as a way to protect oneself.

In forgiveness, we renounce the need for justice and also any wish to explain and understand things completely. There comes a moment when we have to forget about rationalizations and justifications. Justice is not always possible; this can become a trap, and while there is certainly considerable frustration in forgiving without really making oneself understood, it can happen and we have to accept it.

It is important to be extremely careful in how we express forgiveness. We can ask for the other person's forgiveness, but to go to them and tell them we forgive them can all too quickly turn into a settling of scores, justification, feelings of superiority, self-satisfaction, renewed judgment, and it can simply re-open the door to conflict. For the most part, it is enough to forgive inwardly in a clear way and then keep quiet about it; the change of heart will translate into action in one way or another if we are vigilant, in some gesture or look, or some new way of behaving. A disposition to be quiet is a good sign that our heart has been made clean. Experience shows that if we have really forgiven, even if we don't open our mouths, the situation will develop in a totally unexpected way; something will come about over which we have absolutely no control, but that produces the fruit of life.

The act of forgiveness

Once all these steps have been accomplished, the time has come to effect the act of forgiveness. We discover that we are at liberty either to keep the debt or remit it, unravel the situation or keep it as it is, enter a process of setting one or the other party free or remain in chains. But if we do have this clear choice, we cannot indefinitely delay forgiveness. We *can* engage with this mountain pathway that seems insurmountable, but it is the Lord who *will fight for us* (Exod 14:14). In his grace, let's answer the call and *he will deliver us from the hand of the Egyptians* (Exod 14:30).

The act of forgiveness is very specific: "On such and such a day, at such and such a time, I choose to remit this debt. From this day on, you no longer have any debt towards me and I consider you quit." This is accomplished in the deep heart and is a thorough determination. The heart then keeps a record of the transaction, a record to which we can then refer if, as it may, the pain and rebellion is reactivated by chance meetings, conversations, or memories—all of which is perfectly normal. Only, from then on, we know with certainty that this first accomplished act is in effect. Forgiveness has been granted; it is done and we must not go back on our choice. We will simply need to return to it and it will deepen. This is the same process as that involved in a vow of poverty, for example: the forgiveness is an accomplished fact and it will unfold, day by day, often through our spiritual battles.

A stone was cut out without hands; it struck the statue on its feet of iron and clay, and it crushed them (Dan 2:34–35).

CONCLUSION

The Daily Walk of Evangelizing the Depths

I will be with you always
until the end of time.
(Matt 28:20)

If we are happy just to read or to hear teaching on this evangelizing of the depths, we will merely stay on the edge. To have understood and even been greatly interested is not enough. The way has to be walked in day by day, each of us on our own, even though sharing with others and personal counseling are very important. The causes of infected wounds have been seen to, the wounds cleaned, but a daily vigilance is necessary because only if we have a daily walk will restoration take place.

When we have been through some change that seems to have got at the root of things, we can all too easily believe that the matter is done with. However, six months or a year later, it may well be that light will be given us afresh to look at some area of our lives that had been deep in the shadows, and another passage of healing is to follow.

There is, however, a before and an after: our eyes and our ears have been opened. We now have some essential points of reference, and we can now understand what is going on inside us. The birth pains of the new continue, but we are now at peace and trustful.

Life in the Spirit

There is no longer any issue of walking alone. We are sure that the Spirit is there to guide us, that grace strengthens us and is given us every step of the way; we will never lack for anything as we proceed along the interior paths to which we are called.

It is strange to see how some people find themselves frequently brought to a standstill in total helplessness, as if faced by an impassable chasm; it is as if they have completely forgotten that the Spirit can help them. Yes, it is important to be cautious about things that touch on life in the Spirit, and people often take as indications of the Spirit impressions that come from their own psyche. However, this is no reason to be timid or ignorant in this area.

Head for the deep water, said Jesus (Luke 5:4). Dare to do so; get away from the bank, from your old habits. Make an effort to seek grace, learn to recognize it, understand it, take hold of it; learn to consult the Spirit, to listen to him, to understand the way he leads us, and to collaborate with him. The Spirit is alive; Christ is alive. Don't pass by this gift of life.

The spiritual battle

The moment we choose to live and to abandon the ways of death we have known, we can so often think we have reached the end of the matter when we have only just begun. We will have to strengthen, nourish, establish the decision we have made, confirming it day after day and adjusting our behavior in the chosen direction. This means that we are called to engage in a spiritual battle that, indeed, is not a battle between us and God, but a battle together with and in God against darkness (beginning with ourselves). "We are carriers of the life of the Christ, of his victory at the heart of our shadows."[1]

We are, in a way, chosen by God as his partners in this task, and this leads us to *enlarge the space of our tent* (Isa 54:2)—we are not called just to resolve our personal problems but to put ourselves at the service of the great movement of salvation, of the redemption accomplished by Jesus Christ.

Watching prayer

If we really wish to follow this route, we will need to set aside a time each day to go deeper, to be anchored. It's for each of us to find our own rhythm, our own time and place. Do not wait until there is time; it will never arrive.

1. Rosette Genton, oral teaching.

CONCLUSION

There is a question of priorities here. Each day we must go over in prayer, in words, the essence of where we are: go over the word that feeds and builds us, over the things we need to quit, but also over the new step we need to take.

We need to evangelize our behavior and examine, day by day, how we are doing. We mustn't be worried if for a certain period only the negative is apparent: old habits are tenacious. Little by little new behaviors will take their place; the particular word we have been given is a vital support. It will feed our will and light the way.

Each day we are to step out with little acts of freedom. They may seem minimal, but it is essential to believe in their value, since it is thanks to them that our roots strike deep into the ways of life.

Where do we begin?

We can't be working on every level at the same time. We set off from where we are and from what emerges from that, from our lack of well-being, from our reaction to some event. We stay with the area where we discern that the Spirit is at work in us.

According to our need, we must continually go over one or other of the stages of our new pathway. We need to open ourselves to the Spirit anew, take time to experience some particular emotion and allow Christ to come into it, to see if it touches on one of our wounds from the past or one of the mistaken routes we have followed. We must continually rediscover the way out.

Falls

Slips, falls, are normal and inevitable because the wounds are reactivated by events. Nevertheless, often enough, when we are faced with them, we can lose courage because it looks as though the advances we thought we had made were illusory. In fact, we are always tempted by the will to omnipotence and the pursuit of definitive, total healing, when this is not how things work.

We need to know that the process we have been through with Christ, in the Spirit, is firmly anchored and will not be destroyed since it bears the fruit of eternal life. Experience is our reference point; the steps we have taken are real. The root of our wounding has been cleansed, and now we know how to recover from a fall. We know the way. We have only to go over the steps again. Each time we are faced with a difficulty, the Spirit releases new power in us. Far from being a step back, each slip is the occasion for a deepening experience as we overcome it.

We then find, once again, that God's help will never be lacking, in whatever form it takes.

Our pitfalls

One of the most frequent pitfalls for many of us will be the temptation to slip back more permanently. We become aware of our wounds, of the false paths we have taken . . . and then along comes an event that leads us back there, and we fall back into doubt and inertia.

This is to return to the tomb; we have no idea how to fight the essential spiritual fight that is involved here (Deut 30:15–20). We shut ourselves in once more to powerlessness: "What am I going to make of this?" In some strange way, because another aspect to the consequences of our wounds emerges, we don't know how to find the way out. We fail to realize that the seed of resurrection has been planted in us once and for all, that it has woken and began to develop the moment we stepped off the highway of death onto the way of life. It is now, from this moment, given us to enter resurrection life (John 11:25), but on condition that we want it and hold on to that desire.

Nevertheless, it will always be necessary to be coming and going between the present and the past since things that move us deep down in the present will nearly always lead us to one or another of our wounds. It is this that we need be sure to experience in the Spirit, allowing him to guide us through the stages we now know. Then we can rise up and move forward again, courageously carrying our bed.

Further to this, we all have our own pitfalls, our own way of slipping back into the old rut, so we need to know our specific failing and watch. Whenever we fall, we must note how and why we have allowed ourselves to be ensnared.

Spiritual resurrection and physical or psychological healing

There is a difference between spiritual resurrection and the physical or psychological. The ways of evangelizing the depths do not lead only to real spiritual renewal, but also to the mind and emotions being set in order, and the re-establishing or overall improvement in physical health that comes with the redirecting of our energy. We cannot open up every area of our being to the love and light of God without experiencing something very deep in every part.

However, even as we go through this whole process, there may subsist within us deeply rooted, ancient psychological structures, or their resultant physical problems. We need to know this and not torment ourselves in vain, telling ourselves that there is something in us that is not as it should be and that this absolutely has to be healed. Jesus was raised with his scars (John 20:27), and we too will rise with our scars. This is part of being human. This is a very hard reality to accept; it is difficult not to imagine ourselves without limits and not to dream of being immediately and entirely healed. Just because the weaknesses persist, it's not true that we are still experiencing some disorder; no, if we allow the Spirit to bring his light, it then proves possible to live with the weaknesses with a quiet heart and enter into true humility.

No tension

We must watch not to become fixated on too precise an objective. We can succumb to a sort of idolizing of correct thinking and behavior: "Have I understood everything? Do I see all this as I ought to?"

While we need to know our personal points of reference, we also need to throw out rigid expectations and ways of doing things, and enter into the flexibility that characterizes life in the Spirit, following his suggestions, resting in the heart of Christ, accepting our limits.

Gratitude and praise

Every day we must acknowledge the fruits of the way, not thinking of them as insignificant but giving thanks to God again and again.

However, we can go further and become beings of praise. Praise is different to gratitude: we do not give thanks for our disorder or chaos, but we do praise God for all he is, in the certainty that he is at work throughout our lives, including the difficult times. Praise is a little like a magnet that opens the door to love. It enables us to pass from being weighed down and crushed to the confidence and assurance of faith. In itself it is healing since it assumes a turnaround of the heart.

More and more, we glorify God, which is to say we praise him, not only in our heart, but in the way all the parts of our being, of our body and our soul, are being renewed.

In the family

We need to be discreet about our walk, not imposing it on anyone. Each person is free to go his or her own way. Very often we find the first fruits of change to be renunciation of the domination we exercise over the members of our families. If we do this and are in the right place, not demanding that anyone change to meet our views, we will see the family little by little get sorted out. We renounce the idea of helping others according to merely our own wisdom in the way we had done previously. A more humble and truer relationship comes into being. By beginning with ourselves, by undergoing the necessary pathway of deep conversion, we then discover the most authentic way of helping.

Help, counseling

The way is personal and no one else can follow it for us, but it is indispensable that we walk it with trained people who have already travelled down this road to wholeness.

The fruit of our walk can only be proven and expressed in our relationship with others, with our world, since these things are related. All we have been through along the way to our inner land and to the land of our fathers (Gen 31:3) has been given us that we may participate in the construction of what Jesus termed "the kingdom," the renewal of relationship, the giving of self.

Behold I make all things new (Rev 21:5).

BIBLIOGRAPHY

Ancelin-Schützenburger, Anne. *Aïe mes aïeux*. Paris: Epi-La Méridienne, 1993.

Balmary, Marie. *Le Sacrifice interdit*. Paris: Grasset, 1986.

Basset, Lytta. *La joie imprenable*. Geneva: Labor et Fides, 1996.

———. *Le Pardon originel*. Geneva: Labor et Fides, 1995.

Baudiquey, P. Commentary on *The Prodigal Son* by Rembrandt.

Braconnier, Olivier. *Radiographie d'une secte au-dessus de tout soupçon*. Paris: Cerf, 1996. [In the collection "Foi vivante," no. 366, 1996]

Bruguès, Jean-Louis. *Dictionnaire de morale catholique*. Chambray: CLD, 1991.

Buber, Martin. *Le Chemin de l'homme*. Monaco: Rocher, 1991.

Clément, Olivier. *Athanase d'Alexandrie, sources*. Paris: Stock, 1986.

Glardon, Thérèse, et al. *Le Temps pour vivre*. Lausanne: Presses bibliques universitaires, collection "Espace," 1991.

Glardon, Thérèse, Bernard André, and Jean-Claude Schwab in discussion with Hans Bürki. *Le Temps pour vivre*. Lausanne: Presses bibliques universitaires, collection «Espace», 1991.

Hétu, Jean-Luc. *Quelle foi?* Ottawa: Leméac, 1978.

Janton, Pierre. *Cette violence d'abandon qu'est la prière*. Paris: Desclée, 1982.

Lafrance, Jean. *Persévérants dans la prière*. Paris: Médiaspaul, 1962.

Laplace, Jean. *La Prière*. Paris: Centurion, 1974.

Larchet, Jean-Claude. *Thérapeutique des maladies spirituelles*. 1991 and 1993. Reprint. Paris: Cerf, 1997.

Leclerc, Eloi. *Le Royaume caché*. Paris: Desclée De Brouwer, 1987.

Louf, André. *Au gré de sa grâce*. Paris: Desclée De Brouwer, 1989.

———. *Seigneur, apprends-nous à prier*. Bruxelles: Lumen Vitae, 1990.

Nouwen, Henri. *The Return of the Prodigal Son*. London: Darton, Longman and Todd, 1992.

Payne, Leanne. *Crisis in Masculinity*. Westchester, IL: Crossway, 1992.

———. *The Healing Presence: Curing the Soul through Union with Christ*. Grand Rapids: Baker, 1995.

Rondet, Michel. "Dieu a-t-il sur chacun de nous une volonté particulière?" *L'Accompagnement spirituel, Christus* Special issue, 1192.

Sibony, Daniel. *Pour une éthique de l'être*. In *Les Trois Monothéismes*. Paris: Seuil, 1992.

Steinsaltz, Adin. *La Rose aux treize pétales*. Paris: Albin Michel, 1989.

Thérien, Vincent. "Nous avons vu la gloire de Dieu." [unknown citation]

Thévenot, Xavier. *Compter sur Dieu*. Paris: Cerf, 1992.

BIBLIOGRAPHY

————. *Les Péchés, que peut-on en dire?* Mulhouse: Salvator, 1983.

————. *Repères éthiques pour un monde nouveau.* Mulhouse: Salvator, 1982.

————. *Souffrance, bonheur, éthique.* Mulhouse: Salvator, 1990.

Varillon, François. *Joie de croire, joie de vivre.* Paris: Centurion, 1981.

————. *Vivre le christianisme.* Paris: Centurion, 1992.

Vasse, Denis. *Le Temps du désir.* Paris: Seuil, 1969.

Vocabulaire de théologie biblique. Paris: Cerf, 1991.

Winnicott, D. W. "Fear of Breakdown." *The International Review of Psycho-analysis* 1 (1974) 35–44.

CPSIA information can be obtained
at www.ICGtesting.com
Printed in the USA
LVHW091018210520
656170LV00002B/613